A Conversation About Happiness

A Conversation About Happiness

Mikey Cuddihy

Atlantic Books
LONDON

Most names – apart from those of my family, and historically significant ones – have been changed to preserve anonymity. In some cases, characters have been merged. Events are as I remember them, with some fact checking for verification. For the sake of dramatization, timelines have occasionally been altered.

Photographs, my own and family ones (some of them in the public domain), along with Summerhill photos published by Herb Snitzer in his book *Living at Summerhill*, have acted as memory prompts. Some transcripts from Herb's book have also been referred to, and used with Herb's kind permission

First published in trade paperback in Great Britain in 2014 by Atlantic Books, an imprint of Atlantic Books Ltd.

10 9 8 7 6 5 4 3 2 1

A CIP catalogue record for this book is available from the British Library.

Trade Paperback ISBN: 9781782393146
E-book ISBN: 9781782393153

Printed in Sweden by ScandBook AB

Atlantic Books
An Imprint of Atlantic Books Ltd
Ormond House
26–27 Boswell Street
London
WC1N 3JZ

www.atlantic-books.co.uk

For my son, James Cuddihy White

When I close my eyes, I can see her lying in the open coffin surrounded by red roses that cover her feet. She's wearing an ugly wig, too red for her own chestnut hair with an uncharacteristic fringe. She looks strange. I put my hand out to feel if she's real but her skin feels cold, as if she's a waxwork, but not a very good one. I can't equate the woman in the box with my mother. Neither can Sean or my little brother Chrissy. We giggle nervously as we kiss her, each in turn.

Part One

Chapter 1

Uncle Tom picks us up from summer camp in the Catskills, all five of us. That's me, my big sister Deedee, my brothers Bob, Sean and Chrissy. Instead of going home, we drive to the airport where we get on a plane to London for a sightseeing holiday.

I'm quite excited at the prospect of seeing the Queen.

'I don't want to go to England. I want to stay home and play Little League baseball,' screams Sean as Uncle Tom drags him up the steps and hauls him into the plane.

Twenty months older than me, Sean senses that more than a holiday is afoot.

It's late summer 1962. I'm ten years old. Kennedy is in his second year as President and Marilyn Monroe has been found dead in her bedroom from an overdose. I arrive at Heathrow in just the clothes I'm standing in: a pair of shorts and a candy-striped cotton shirt with chocolate ice-cream stains down the front. I'm clutching a white calico dachshund under my arm with the autographs of all the friends I've made during our six weeks at Camp Waneta. I rub my legs to combat the chill and walk uncertainly down the metal steps, squinting out at a drizzly grey sky.

They say Mom never regained consciousness. November 1961 and it's raining. My mother turns a corner too sharply and the family Packard skids on fallen leaves. The car hits the tree. Mom goes straight through the windscreen, the steering wheel crushing her chest.

There are rumours amongst my older siblings that Mom had been on the verge of leaving my stepfather. Perhaps her death hadn't been an accident. Another rumour has it that she'd started drinking again so was driving erratically or maybe, they speculated, she was so dosed up on tranquillizers that her reflexes were bad. My big brother Bob blames my stepfather or 'the Gooper', as he calls him behind his back, for being too mean to have the car fixed. One of the doors was tied shut with an old piece of washing line and he knew that the brakes were dodgy.

We all blame ourselves to some extent.

Our father died four years earlier in his own car accident, driving a much racier Ford Coupé.

Five years old, I put on a new dress my stepmother has made me. I go into the living room to show him my dress. Daddy has come home from work and is sitting in his comfortable Ezy-Rest armchair, ice cubes clinking in his whisky glass.

I do a twirl for him.

'Very nice.' Daddy gives an approving smile, pats me on the head, and I toddle off happily to get ready for bed.

I'm puzzled when I wake in the morning to be told that Daddy is dead. He died on his way home from the city. But I had seen him with my own eyes just last night.

So now we're orphans.

This is where Uncle Tom steps in, setting the wheels in motion to adopt us. My father comes from a huge, Irish-Catholic family who have done extremely well in publishing on one side (Funk and Wagnalls, The Literary Digest), and inventing on the other (his grandfather was the millionaire inventor, T. E. Murray). He's one of five brothers and two sisters who adored him; he was a tearaway, the black sheep, or Robert the Roué, as they affectionately called him, later shortened to 'Roo'.

Uncle Tom has the same good looks as our father; his dark hair made even darker with Brylcreem, the same wry, gentle smile, a fatherly way of patting me on the head. With his soft authoritative voice, the Manhattan accent with the flattened vowels, he even sounds like Daddy. It's difficult to tell them apart in photos, so he's a fitting stand in as far as we're concerned. Tom jokes that he's 'drawn the short straw' when he takes us on, and I imagine my uncles sitting in my grandmother's Park Avenue apartment drawing straws from someone's hands – perhaps Arthur, the butler, proffering the straws like fancy hors d'oeuvres.

Uncle Tom studied economics at Harvard and went into investment banking, but after three children and a messy divorce at the age of thirty he dropped out, returning to university to take a PhD in psychology.

My sister says he kidnapped us.

Deedee is called into the principal's office at her high school one lunchtime: 'Edith, your uncle is here to see you.'

Deedee hasn't seen Uncle Tom for a long time. He takes her out for lunch, to Herb McCarthy's, a sophisticated bar and grill in town. She orders her favourite thing, a grilled cheese sandwich and a Coca-Cola.

'How would you like to come and live with me here in Southampton? I've rented a place on Herrick Road just around the corner from your school.'

My sister is thinking: *Uncle Tom looks rich. His plan sounds like a load of fun. Maybe I'll get my very own Princess telephone.*

'Yes, OK,' she says. 'But what about the others, and Larry, and Mimmy?'

'I've squared it with them, don't you worry!' (Of course he hasn't.)

'I'll send a car to pick you up after school, and your sister and little brothers. You can move in straightaway.'

My brother, Bob, holds out for a while, loyal to Mimmy, my mother's mother, and even to my stepfather, Larry, whom he had reviled when my mother was alive. But he knows it's hopeless, and anyway, sharing a house with Uncle Tom seems like a better proposition than living with our exhausted stepfather and our frail and crotchety grandma.

Our new house is a lovely shingle affair with a porch. It's located on one of the prettier streets behind the Presbyterian Church in town, not far from school. Uncle Tom indulges our every whim.

Mine is that I want to be called Elizabeth, my middle name, instead of Mikey, named for my father's favourite brother, Michael, who was struck down with polio at the age of nineteen. This is occasionally lengthened to Michael when my sister is angry with me.

Tom installs a kind black couple, George and Lessie-May, to look after us during the week – he's working in the city weekdays – and so now we're all set. But one of us is missing – my half-sister, Nanette, and although I have my own very nice room in a clean and ordered house, my little sister isn't here. She's only four and a half years old and she belongs to my stepfather, so he keeps her.

At weekends, Uncle Tom makes us do inkblot tests, ten little cards invented by someone called Rorschach. They remind me of the flash cards in kindergarten, with a picture of an apple, or a dog, where you have to say what it is. This time, there are shapes – blobby and symmetrical.

'Tell me what you see,' says Tom.

Is this a trick question?

'Rabbits, twin baby elephants, an angel, butterflies. Gosh, maybe a couple of Russian Cossacks… dancing wearing red hats.'

'Good,' says Tom.

He seems pleased with my answers. He appears pensive, sometimes a little surprised-looking, but there never seems to be a wrong answer. I like the Rorschach test better than the kindergarten flash cards. They're more interesting.

The first thing Tom does to make his claim for custody more viable is quickly to marry a girlfriend of his, Joan Harvey. Joan is beautiful and funny and an actress. She stars in the popular TV soap, *The Edge of Night*. She devises ways of saying hello to us when she's on TV.

One morning when she's leaving for the city, she says, 'Watch for me touching my right ear, that'll mean I'm saying hi.'

We rush home from school, take our peanut butter and jelly sandwiches and glasses of milk to the living room, and scrutinize the television. Sure enough, at the given moment she gives the signal. We whoop with delight.

Uncle Tom has had a wealthy and privileged upbringing, but it's also been conservative and religious. The boys were sent away to Benedictine boarding schools, my father to a Catholic military academy run by Jesuits, and the girls to the Convent of the Sacred Heart. My brother Bob, aged fifteen, is at the same military establishment and my sister spent a term at Kenwood, a Catholic boarding school in Albany, New York, before returning to our local high school. We three younger kids have so far escaped these types of schools, my mother opting instead for the local elementary. God only knows what my wealthy grandmother had in store for us.

My Uncle Tom wants us to have something better, in England, where we'll be able to make a fresh start, leave the past behind and begin again.

The thing is, he isn't coming with us.

When Uncle Tom shows up at Camp Waneta, I haven't seen him for over a month. He takes us out to a diner in town. Acker Bilk's

'Stranger on the Shore' is playing on the jukebox. The tune is the background melody to the summer; it seems to be playing wherever we go. I make up words, singing along to the plaintive clarinet solo in my head:

> *I don't know why, I love you like I do;*
> *I don't know why I do; I do, I do I do.*
> *The birds that sing their song,*
> *Are singing just for you.*
> *I don't know why I love; I do, I do, I do.*

Uncle Tom has a camera with him and wants to take photos of us. He gets us to pose, individually, not together like a happy family.

'Deedee, can you stand over there, against the sky. I need you on a pale background. Good. Mikey, you next.'

I smile as best I can.

'Well, kids, I guess that just about wraps it up for the time being. See you in a couple a weeks.' And off he goes.

Sure enough, two weeks later, Uncle Tom comes to get us in a big station wagon. My Aunt Joan is with him. There's lots of luggage in the back. There are five duffel bags, each with our names written in heavy marker pen on the straps. I've been looking forward to seeing my little sister Nanny, my Grandma Mimmy and my toys, but we don't drive home like I expect. We drive straight to Idlewild airport and on to the plane.

As usual Uncle Tom is accompanied by an entourage of strange men. Seven of them have come to see him off. Saul, a grey-haired man who seems to be in charge, is giving Uncle Tom an injection. Standing on the runway, my uncle has his sleeve rolled up. He's afraid of flying. So am I, but I'm afraid of injections too, so I keep quiet.

My uncle's friends take turns to hug him and pat him on the back.

'You can do it, Tommy, have courage,' they say, which is puzzling, because we're only going to England for a week.

Joan doesn't come with us.

When I ask her what she will be doing, and won't she be lonely without us, she says, 'Don't worry, I'll stay home and play with myself.'

My older brothers and my sister laugh, as if she's told a very funny joke. Then my Uncle Tom hands out our passports with the photos taken at Camp Waneta, against the pale blue sky.

In London, we stay in a little hotel off Leicester Square. We do a lot of sightseeing by taxi and throw water bombs from the fifth-floor window of the hotel. We go and see *West Side Story* at the Odeon, where a woman gives me a box of almost uneaten Maltesers. My sister teases me that they are poisoned. The little balls of chocolate roll around in their box temptingly, and in spite of the danger, I eat them all, waiting until one chosen chocolate sphere and its magical centre has melted on my tongue before putting a fearful hand inside the box to take another, and another.

And then, quite abruptly, the holiday is over.

The strange thing is we don't go home.

My uncle takes me and my brothers Sean and Chrissy (twenty-three months younger than me) to a train station. I can just make out the letters over the entrance. Liverpool Street Station. A kind lady with a foreign accent meets us. My uncle shakes her hand and introduces us.

Tom says, 'Don't worry, I'll be over to see you at Christmas. We'll all be together then.'

We've already said goodbye to Bob and Deedee at the hotel; they are going to a school in Scotland, called Kilquhanity.

What a funny name, I think.

My sister says, 'Don't worry, Mikey, we'll see each other on vacation, and I'll write you a letter.'

I haven't had a letter before.

My sister is quite excited. She finds the constant change kind of addictive. She's thinking: *This'll be fun. My friends are going to be so jealous.*

And yes, there is something exciting about this big adventure. But being shunted around, the secrecy, the unpredictability of it all has begun to wear a bit thin.

'OK, kids, I want you to be good. Do what the lady tells you and run along with her, the porter has your luggage. He'll take you to your carriage.'

Carriage as in *Cinderella*?

My uncle gives his slightly wry smile. He ruffles my brothers' hair and kisses me on the forehead. The lady takes my hand. I've never been on a train before. I'm too excited to feel sad. There have been so many goodbyes anyway and there is probably something nice to look forward to at the end of this journey.

Uncle Tom waves until we are out of view. I put my calico dog up to the window so he can see out, and I get him to wave his paw. Sean is too defeated to fight this time. He is standing, leaning with his chin on his folded arms, against the window next to a sign that reads, 'Do not lean out of the window.'

I feel sorry for him. There's an ocean between him and his Little League baseball now. 'Sean, be careful,' I plead with him.

He sits down, heavily.

The engine and the steam and the noise lull us into silence. We look out of the window at the grey city going by and then we slow down as we cross a bridge, high above a little street of doll-like terraces, with front doors opening right onto the pavement. The bridge runs across the middle, dividing the street in half. The houses aren't very far below and I can see a group of children playing hopscotch; others are skipping; a small child is riding a tricycle along the pavement. A mother stops to shield her eyes and look up at our train. It seems like she's looking straight at me. I wave and the woman waves back. The children and the woman disappear from view as the train moves on, and I can see the backs of the houses now, washing on some of the lines, white sheets, and then big grey buildings, factories, and the train gets faster, faster and then I fall asleep.

When I wake up, there is green going past the window, and

beyond, flat yellow fields and little square towers and lots of sky with frothy clouds that seem to mimic the green foliage. The kind lady with the foreign accent is knitting. I'm fascinated. She doesn't knit like my granny Mimmy, with the right hand looping the wool over the left hand needle. She keeps the wool stretched tightly around her left forefinger, and stabbing the right-hand needle into the wool. Every once in a while she stops to count her stitches in a language I don't understand.

'*Zwei, drei, vier, fünf, sechs.*'

She's very fast.

Chapter 2

'Who's that funny old man with the dog?' I ask a freckle-faced girl who looks like she knows her way around.

I keep seeing a tall man in a brown corduroy jacket and baggy old man's jeans, the kind that carpenters wear. On his feet are enormous shiny black lace-ups. He's stooped and has a strange accent. I think he must be German.

He's surrounded by a group of small children who are jumping up at him, shouting, 'Neill! Neill!'

He looks down, keeping a lighted cigarette out of their way.

'You, you and you, go and find me a great big man with white hair who's been seen wandering around the school. He's an awfully nice-looking chap!'

'It's you! It's you! You're the man with the white hair!' they all shout, laughing excitedly.

Evie turns to me and smiles: 'Oh, that's Neill. This is *his* school.'

'What, you mean he's the principal?'

'I guess, well, the headmaster, but not like a normal head.

I mean, he doesn't order us around or tell us what to do.'

'So, does he just kind of hang around?'

'I guess so. Sometimes he says things at the meeting, but he has to put his hand up and wait for the chairman to call his name before he can speak, like everyone else.'

'Oh,' I say, still a little puzzled.

I'm assigned a dormitory on the first floor, a big room with bare floorboards, and a rusty fire escape leading from one of the gabled windows at the side. There are five other girls: one American, three English, and one Norwegian. My new family consists of sixty kids and a few adults, mostly foreign, all displaced, trying to figure out how to live in Neill's self-constructed, child-centred universe.

We sleep in old army bunks. The school had been evacuated during the war and taken over as an army HQ (given its proximity to the Suffolk coastline it's perhaps unsurprising). The war is something remote and we're not sure when it finished. It could've been last week for all we know. There are reminders everywhere: sandpits, bunkers, look-out posts on the beach at Sizewell. I hear people talking about something called rationing. I can't imagine not being allowed sweets if you have the money to pay for them. Wooden huts with flat, corrugated iron roofs serve as classrooms and sleeping quarters for the staff. These are heated (unlike the big house) with fumy paraffin stoves, which we children huddle over as we scribble with ancient ballpoint pens, in equally ancient and mouldy exercise books (also army surplus).

I get a top bunk perhaps because I am tall and thin and can hoist myself up easily. Below me is Vicky Gregory, from Portland, Oregon. She has a big sister and a little brother here too. Vicky is loud and robust with a good sense of humour; she has what the English call a cheeky grin.

All our parents are absent, only mine are dead.

Vicky's parents are psychiatrists: 'My dad came to America from Russia when he was three on a passenger ship. His grandma looked like a Russian babushka, you know, with a shawl wrapped over her head, and a long dress. She couldn't speak a word of English. My mom's a Native American. She worked in a hospital that's been written about in a book!' (*One Flew Over the Cuckoo's Nest* will be filmed a decade later.)

Next to our bunk a single bed will be added for Anna, who arrives from California the following term. A shy, pale, softly spoken girl with golden-coloured hair and a nagging cough.

On the other side of the room, in a top bunk, is Evie (with the freckles), an old-timer. She's been at Summerhill since she was four. Evie is proud of her status and can always be relied upon to fill us in on school traditions.

'Do you know how to play fuck-chase?' is pretty much her first question to me.

I have difficulty imagining fuck-chase actually working. Little boys with their limp baby penises chasing little girls and then bumping up against them ineffectually. Perhaps the other way round, the girls chasing the boys, would be more viable.

'We're not a school-school,' says Evie, parroting Neill's speech made earlier that week. 'We're a *community* and we all have an equal say in how things are run. We can do whatever we like, as long as it doesn't harm anyone.'

Apparently we have freedom, but we don't have *licence*, whatever this means.

Eleanor from London sleeps on the bottom bunk; her little brother Hector is at the school too. She has dirty blonde hair held back with an increasingly grubby velvet headband, and round, pink, National Health specs. She speaks like the Queen with a pronounced upper-class accent, hangs out with the older boys, and is considered a bit of a swot.

Diagonal to their bunk is Hannah from Hammersmith. Hannah's parents, Daphne and Robert, have sent her to several schools, including the French Lycée, and she still can't read. Today, she would be diagnosed as dyslexic. In despair, her parents have sent her to Summerhill, where at least she's happy. One day Hannah will become a renowned china restorer, but right now she is amazingly clumsy with the 'wrong' kind of hair, unfashionably curly and frizzy.

Hannah's mother – who looks like a more chic version of Princess Margaret (big sunglasses, orange lipstick and a silk scarf tied fashionably behind her head) – sends weekly copies of *Bunty* and *Judy*. These are bagsied and passed around. Gosh, it's awful being tenth in line, the comic tattered and out of date by the time it reaches you. Hannah's parents also send expensive biscuits for her birthday, from Harrods – chocolate florentines, the chocolate too grown-up and bitter for us to gorge on, and glacéed chestnuts which are equally disgusting.

On the top bunk, above Hannah, is Vaar from Norway. Vaar is the exotic one. Her mother, an African American, is an opera singer and sang in the first ever production of *Porgy and Bess*. She was the first African American to study at the Julliard School, but gave up her career in America to marry a Norwegian skiing champion. Vaar has black, curly hair and almond eyes. She can climb trees like a monkey and mostly hangs out with the boys. She wears Norwegian sweaters patterned with snowflakes, and ski pants, but she also wears a black leather jacket when she's tree climbing, which gives her a boyish edge. Her parents send her parcels with amber-coloured cheese, which she cuts with a special cheese knife. Shaving thin, semi-transparent slices from the block, she hands out slivers, like sweets.

Lying in our beds in the dark, away from our families, we talk about home.

Evie brags about her mother Myrtle:

'She once appeared on a TV programme called *Six-Five Special* with her skiffle group. Dad doesn't live with us. He's a famous actor. He's with the RSC, and he's been in Ealing Comedies.'

I don't ask what they are.

'Tell us about your mom.' Vicky's voice rises up through the dark.

'Oh,' I hesitate, feeling my way into Mom's room. 'She had so many dresses. I guess my favourite was the black and orange one with a black velvet bodice and a skirt and collar in orange silk…'

I run my fingers over the fabric on the skirt as Mom busies herself with her stockings. I watch her fish out an unladdered pair from the scramble of froth in her underwear drawer, and attach them to the stubby and exhausted-looking straps that dangle from the bottom of the girdle.

'Can I look in your jewellery box?' I ask her.

She passes it over. I pull out long strands of beads and untangle them. Matching up her earrings, I lay them out on the counterpane.

Mom is getting dressed. She is wearing a strange undergarment, a Playtex Living Girdle. It isn't actually alive, but apparently it *breathes*. The girdle, coupled with her Playtex Living Bra, to keep her saggy breasts pert and pointing forward, makes her look like a slightly under-done mermaid. The ribbed white fabric of the girdle, with its diamond shape panel of satin at the front, starts at her ribs, finishing at the tops of her thighs.

'Good grief, I can't believe the time,' says Mom.

It's late afternoon and people are coming over for cocktails. Mom is going to wear one of her hostess gowns, which button down the front so you don't need to wait for your husband to come home from work to help you with the zip. Mom has a collection of hostess gowns. They combine the glamour of a cocktail dress with the practicality of a housecoat. Somehow Mom always manages to look classy. It doesn't matter if the dress comes from Saks Fifth Avenue or John's Bargain Store. Everything looks good on her. And she still has some nice jewellery left over from when we were rich and she was married to my father.

'Then what?' says Vaar.

My mind skips forward to the time when my stepfather locked my mother in the bedroom and poured all the booze down the toilet. In revenge or desperation, Mom drank the bottle of Chanel No. 5 that was sitting on her dressing table.

'Mom and Larry once had this awful fight. Mom stormed out and we drove to Montauk. Just the two of us,' I say.

What bliss to have her all to myself, just this once. To have the front seat where I can play with the cigarette lighter; pushing it in on the dashboard so that, when you pull it out, the end is glowing a bright red, coiled circle. Driving the five miles into town, most of the countryside is flat, but there is a hilly road that Mom speeds up for. It makes my tummy flip with excitement. The Roller Coaster Road, we call it.

Usually, the Packard is stuffed with kids. Without warning, Mom will turn and swat us with her free hand.

'Stop your squabbling.'

We're in town, in the car park outside Bohack's grocery store, and she is trying to get Sean into the car. He wants to stay and play baseball with his friend Davey Crockett and my mother is swatting him, and missing. She's slurring her words, shouting: 'Get in the God darn car, Sean.'

People are looking at us. I'm embarrassed. I want her to stop.

'Stop it. Just stop it, you drunken fucking bastard!'

My mother does stop. So does my brother. He looks at me:

You are in so much trouble, Mikey. More trouble than me.

My mother gets everyone into the car – well, Sean and Chrissy, my little sister, all the groceries in their brown paper bags – and she drives off without me. I'm left, standing in the middle of the car park. I wait a little while to see if she will turn around and come and get me. Surely she'll turn around. I'm only eight years old. Surely she wouldn't leave a child on her own to walk home? There is no sign of the Packard; I know the way home, and I start walking. I walk past the brown shingled Methodist Church, past Herb McCarthy's Bar and Grill, past the road to the railway station, until I reach the edge of town – no houses, and just a grass verge with a fork in the road. I'm not entirely sure of the way now; I guess I just have to keep walking, straight ahead. Soon, some neighbours – the Johnsons who live nearby – stop in their car and give me a lift.

My brothers are in the living room, watching the *Howdy Doody* show on television. There's no sign of Mom. I go upstairs to her room. The curtains are closed. She doesn't tell me off because she is lying on her bed, crying like a little girl.

I stand there: 'Mommy. I'm sorry, Mommy, I didn't mean it. I'm sorry I swore at you, Mommy.'

'You're right, Michael, I AM a drunk. But "fucking bastard". How COULD you? Don't you know a fucking bastard is the most beautiful thing in the world? Don't you ever forget that,' she says through angry tears.

I wish I could undo my words. I'm trying to work out whether she's angry about the swearing or the misuse of fucking bastard.

I'm confused. She's still crying. The bed is shaking with her sobs.

'Can I get you anything, Mommy?' I wish there was something I could get her.

'No, dear, I'll be all right. I just need a few minutes to myself.'

Sure enough, pretty soon she has her apron on and she's in the kitchen, clattering pots and pans, as she cooks spaghetti sauce for dinner. Our favourite.

Communal living, after six weeks of Camp Waneta, doesn't seem that strange to me. Perhaps I'm in a state of shock. During our first few weeks, Chrissy and I play on a deserted bit of land just outside the school perimeter. It's an old army manoeuvre area with sweet-smelling gorse bushes dotted about in the sandy soil. We wander through it, eyes squinting in the darkening afternoon, searching.

'Mom?'

We run after her, but her ghost eludes us, disappearing into the shadows.

That night my mother suddenly appears at the school to collect us in the Packard.

'It's all been a terrible mistake,' she says, climbing out of the car, unscathed, to gather us into her arms.

She hasn't died after all, and no, this isn't a dream, I am actually awake – this is real.

And then I wake up.

Chrissy and I spend a lot of time sitting on the wall that marks the boundary of the school, 'Summerhill' painted along it in plain white capitals. We've heard the grown-ups talking about the Cuban missile crisis. Something is being decided back home, battled out between our President and Khrushchev, but no one tells us anything. We sit, gazing out at the gravel drive, wondering if we're all about to die, far away from home, exiled on this cold island of damp crisps and salad cream. I have no urge to run away. I'm just waiting for someone to show up.

We begin to make our own friends. I only see my brothers at mealtimes or in the Saturday General Meetings. The General Meeting is where grievances, petty and grave, are aired. For a 'free' school, where children can do what they like, there are a lot of rules. Pages of them, all written by the school council and pinned to the notice board on one of the panelled walls in the lounge.

I try my best to be kind to Sean whenever I bump into him.

'Hi Seanie, how're things?'

'Crap. I'm just waiting to get thrown out of this place so they can send me home'

I have a feeling *home* doesn't exist anymore, this is it, but I don't want to disillusion him.

'Really? But you haven't done anything really bad.'

I miss Deedee with her dark hair and deep brown eyes. Perhaps if Deedee were with us, things would be different. At school in America, she protected me from the bullies who threw their sneakers from the top of the changing room door, and the girl at Camp Waneta who made me cry. She was good at telling my brothers off too. But torn apart, we have to create our own little worlds, overseen by our respective housemothers.

The housemothers each have their own group of similarly aged children. They look after our practical needs and give the little ones a cuddle when they are feeling homesick. Once a week they present us with a neat pile of ironed clothing with our name tags sewn inside: vest, pants, jeans (increasingly patched), a shirt and pyjamas.

Sean has Olly (real name Daphne Oliver) who is fat and jolly and plays the trombone. She dresses in men's clothing, usually a plaid shirt and carpenter's jeans, has short black hair, highlighted with grey as the years go by, and apple-red cheeks. She laughs a lot, in a way that's almost like crying, with her eyes completely closed. She runs the school jazz band. They play 'trad' jazz because that's what she loves. Her hero is someone called Kid Ory. Chrissy will soon come to play the tea-chest bass quite convincingly; he really puts his heart into it.

Chrissy has a succession of house mothers, before he moves up to Olly and 'the Carriages' (a separate building made from old railway carriages, huddled around a coal burner). Luckily for me, I'm handed over to the foreign lady who met us at the train station in London. I don't know it yet, but Ulla will become the centre of my world.

Chapter 3

I wonder why I didn't see this coming. I mean, only a few months ago, I was at my Uncle's place in New York with Deedee who was lying on the couch, reading a book.

'What are you reading?'

She flashes the cover: *Summerhill: A Radical Approach to Child Rearing* by A.S. Neill.

'It's about a school in England.'

'What's that?'

'A free school. You can do what you like. The kids run the school and you don't have to go to classes if you don't want to.'

'Is that good?'

'Listen to this,' she says to her boyfriend (her feet are on his lap). "Sex with love is the greatest pleasure in the world, and it is repressed because it is the greatest pleasure."'

She looks at him significantly.

Doug is older than my sister. He's interested in the Beat poets and has even been to Europe. The idea of a 'free school' appeals to them both. They've recently returned from a trip to Greenwich Village where they mingled with the beatniks in Washington Square, wearing dark glasses and blue jeans.

She goes on flicking through the pages: '"Punishment is an act of hate. Summerhill is possibly the happiest school in the world. I seldom hear a child cry, because children who are free have much less hate to express than children who are downtrodden. At Summerhill we treat children as equals. Each member of the teaching staff and each child, regardless of his age, has one vote."'

'Cool,' says Doug.

'It's all very well,' says my sister, 'but I can't see that working in practice.' (At fourteen and a half she is already a sceptic.) 'What would you do with yourself all day?' she wonders out loud. 'I like being told what to do. I mean, come on – a six-year-old having the same authority as the principal!'

She goes on, reading out the final paragraph '"How can happiness be bestowed? Abolish authority… Let the child be himself. Don't teach him… Don't force him to do anything." Wow,' she says, and she slams the book shut like a big full stop.

My uncle quizzes us.

'How would you kids like to go to this school in England?'

'Could I take my toys?' I ask. 'Would we sail to England on a boat?'

I can't imagine sleeping at the school, at least not at the weekends. Surely we would be living with my aunt and uncle and my little sister, and maybe even George and Lessie-May? In a big house near Buckingham Palace, perhaps.

'I think it sounds stupid,' says my sister.

Deedee has her boyfriend and access to my uncle's charge account, should she want new clothes. She's happy in spite of losing Mom and the fact that Uncle Tom has put a lock on the telephone. I'm not sure how my brothers feel about it.

The subject is dropped and never discussed again until Uncle Tom drops his bombshell. We're not going home. We're going to Summerhill, or at least Sean, Chrissy and myself are.

Summerhill won't accept pupils over the age of twelve.

'Neill thinks the damage has been done by then,' says Uncle Tom. 'Bob and Deedee are going to Kilquhanity.' (The Scottish school in the borders inspired by Summerhill.)

This doesn't feel like an explanation. It just opens up more questions. What does he mean by *damage*? What's happened to them to cause the damage?

Of course, I don't ask.

I have a sense that Neill is bemused by us, the new Americans, who've arrived following the success of his American bestseller, *Summerhill*. Overnight, or so it seems, the school intake has more than doubled. And everyone's speaking with an American accent. Sometimes, for fun, Neill talks to us in American gangster slang with a Scottish lilt. It's an out of date slang that belongs to black and white, 1930s movies starring Edward G. Robinson and James Cagney.

'D'ya wanna sock on the button?'

We dance around him, laughing.

'Gimme the dough or I'll fill ya full of lead!'

'Say it again! Say it again!'

We are a new kind of American child – different from the Americans he'd encountered when he first visited the US in the optimistic 1940s, just after the war. Since the dark days of 1950s McCarthyism, he hasn't been allowed to return because of his friendship with Wilhelm Reich, who he met in Oslo in 1937 when he was invited to lecture at Norway University. Neill was a great admirer of Reich's books, *The Sexual Revolution*, *Character Analysis* and *The Function of the Orgasm*. In fact, Neill went on to study under Reich and agreed to undertake Vegetotherapy, which involved lying naked on a sofa while Reich attacked his stiff muscles. (This I learn from a book years later.)

This is the 1960s. We're part of the new wave of spoilt brats whose counter-cultural, media mogul parents have interpreted freedom rather differently from Neill. We haven't experienced the privations of war and rationing like the English and the Europeans. But Neill needs us; we are *his* bread and butter, his salvation.

Our days at Summerhill are endless, structured only by mealtimes, the ringing of the bell for breakfast, lunch, dinner, and bedtime, and the weekly meeting where we discuss general issues. The rest of the time is ours to do what we like with: playing jacks in the corridor, families in the woods, and (for me, anyway) reading. My favourite book lives in Ulla's room. It is a little hardbound volume, *Fashion through the Ages*. I pore over the illustrated plates, taking in the nuance and detail of empire-line dresses from the early 1800s and their evolution to Victorian corsetry and bustles, on through to the Edwardian period, where the hems are raised to show a bit of ankle, and finishing at drop-waist flapper dresses in the 1920s.

I swap my American Nancy Drew mysteries for two books by Erich Kästner – also in Ulla's room: *Emil and the Detectives* where the children in the illustrations wear strange clothes – the boys in knickerbockers and big lace-up boots – and get about in old-fashioned cars, with running boards, clunky bicycles; and *Lottie and Lisa*, about identical twins who are brought up separately, and meet by accident when they are older.

The school has a library of sorts, a small, wood-panelled room off the lounge with a tattered armchair, unlit fireplace (with graffiti carved around the wooden edges) and a few shelves of old books. Someone called Enid Blyton seems to have written most of them. For a long time I think her first name is 'Cnid' until someone says it to me. The child detectives, *The Famous Five*, all seem rather prissy and dull to me.

Here at Summerhill, I've been looking forward to lessons. But they aren't compulsory. This means you don't have to go. You can play all day if you want to. On the other hand, you can go to any lessons you want. It's kind of like a pick and mix.

Back at home, on Long Island, I liked school. As a homage to my dead father, or perhaps to soothe his grieving mother, Mom sends us to the local Catholic school. I have a sweet teacher with a boy's name, just like me, with a girl's name at the end: Sister John Marie.

She wears a full nun's habit, like all the teachers, but she is young and pretty. There is a statue of the Virgin Mary in our classroom, and we sing a lovely song to her: O *Mary, we crown thee with blossoms today, Queen of the Angels, Queen of the May…*

Sister John draws a circle in white chalk on the squeaky blackboard.

'This represents your soul.'

Every time you sin, a mark goes onto the soul (squeaky chalk sound) until it's filled up (lots of frantic white marks inside the circle). When you go to confession and say your rosary afterwards, those sins are wiped away (she has a special wooden block with thick grey felt stuck onto one side that she uses for this task), and your soul is cleansed.

I can't help noticing that the circle is a little smudged, not as pristine as it was before the sins were added.

We are instructed to write letters, prayers or wishes to the Virgin Mary. Sister John Marie shows us how to fold our pieces of paper into a clever envelope and then we go outside to the play-ground and burn the letters on a bonfire. I'm a little reticent about throwing my letter into the flames; it has taken me a long time to write my message down, as I have only been reading and writing, properly for a little while.

But I watch the frilly black and grey ashes, peppered with little flecks of fire, rise up to heaven, smoke billowing, pushing the prayers up and up, until they disappear into the blue sky and out of sight, for ever. I imagine Mary, on her cloud, receiving the wishes, graciously, serenely, looking down at us with heavily lidded eyes. And it is here, with the nuns, that I realize the importance of writing things down, so that they become fixed. True.

At my first confession I make up some sins.

'Father, I've said "shut up" three times this week and "darn" once.'

'Now, Michael, you must say three Hail Marys and one Our Father on your rosary.'

This is when the nightmares begin. I'm going to burn in hell in a pot of boiling oil.

So, Mom takes me out of school. The other children are pages ahead of me when we read together from our Dick and Jane books: *See Spot Run. Run Spot, Run.* I can't grasp the concept of reading. It all seems so complicated, the letters on the page a curious kind of hieroglyphics, or secret code. Eventually, at home, Deedee sits me down and shows me how the individual letters have their own individual sound, and when grouped together, they form a word. I'm ecstatic and become an avid reader.

When I'm sent back to school, it's a different school with a flag above the blackboard and every day we pledge allegiance to the United States of America. I never say very much. I'm not good at raising my hand to answer a questions, even when I'm 100 per cent sure of the answer. There's no knowing if I might stammer and set my classmates off into sniggers.

I want to blame my mother.

'You'll grow out of it,' she used to say.

Why did I believe her?

Instead she died, leaving me with my stammer. I feel my face contort as I try to get out a difficult syllable, neck clenched, fists in a ball. I feel people look away or I suffer the humiliation of having them try and guess the word or the ending of a sentence for me. I can never say what I really want to; the right words elude me; they hold a power that I can't articulate, so I resort to writing.

The stammer shapes all of my decisions – it defines everything about me. Except when I paint or draw or sing. Then I'm fluent, free from hesitancy. I can do almost nothing that involves speaking without it being an ordeal. Asking for a ticket on the bus, I always try to have the right change, in case, when it came to the dreaded moment, I won't be able to ask for the fare. In shops, I point to things, rather than ask.

(Later on, I discover that I never stammer when I'm drunk or lose my temper; shouting helps the flow of words. I allow these two things to happen every once in a while to relieve the tension, but I feel a terrible sense of shame afterwards, as I go around, apologizing, which again is an agony of stuttering and explanation.)

The stammer is, in effect, a disability. In fact, it's not until I'm twenty-seven that I decide the stammer is not going to go away. I'm not going to grow out of it, as my mother had promised. So I go to see a speech therapist who manages, through a series of relaxation exercises and behaviour therapy, to help me overcome the worst of it, or at least to gain more control over my speech.

Why did nobody ever think of this before?

But that is over a decade away.

Chapter 4

My housemother Ulla has offered to teach me French. Ulla is German so English is her second language but Ulla is something of a linguist. Ulla teaches me from a nineteenth-century exercise book, based on Linette, Ninette and Minette, three French chickens. The books have beautiful line-drawing illustrations. Later she will teach me how to read guitar music from an ancient German book. The first song I learn is 'Wooden Heart'. The words sound nothing like Elvis's but the tune is the same:

> *Muss I denn, muss I denn,*
> *Zum stadtele hinaus,*
> *Stadtele hinaus*
> *Und du mein schatz bleibest hier*

Every month, *Grazia,* a sophisticated Italian fashion magazine, is delivered to her. I devour the glossy photos of the models in their glamorous outfits, matching hats and gloves, and the exotic-looking words, all ending in uplifting vowels. Together we explore the dramatic arrivals on the catwalk, in Italian.

'*La moda, amore, qualcosa…*' I stretch my mouth around the words.

I read aloud the elegant headline in capital letters on the cover of the magazine: "'*ALL'UNCINETTO COLLETTI NOVIA' PER LA SERA*." Ulla, what does this mean?'

'Oh, that. Novelty crochet collar for the evening.'

The English translation is often disappointing.

'*Doppio brodo.*' I point to an article inside the magazine.

'Double broth. A kind of soup. Now stop pestering me, I'm trying to fix this bit of sewing that has gone wrong for the little one here.'

Sometimes, for special occasions and parties, Ulla wears a dirndl, a bodice with a skirt and apron across the front. It's rather girlish looking.

Ulla's not the only German at Summerhill – there's also Harry Herring, our art teacher: tall, handsome, middle-aged, rather remote. Harry's studio and living quarters are at the side of the old coach house, or theatre; a high-raftered ceiling, covered in cobwebs, with stacks of old paintings, canvases, sculpture. It's a forbidden and rather fascinating lair. Harry is a man of few words. At the end of term, he always does a mime act, the same one every time. First of all, he mimes eating a banana – you can almost believe he's peeling and then eating an invisible banana. Then he holds his hands out in front of him – palms facing the audience, and feels his way across an imaginary plate glass window. He's very convincing.

I notice Ulla doesn't seem to want to have much to do with Harry; I'm not sure why. But Neill likes to practise his German and I catch him in conversation with her, '*Ja, Ich bin ein Berliner…*', a passing couple of words.

Everything about Ulla fascinates me. She came to England from Berlin in the 1930s to work as an au pair. When the Reichstag was burnt down, she decided not to return. Neill took her in as the cook, but soon realized that cooking wasn't her forte. She has a wardrobe which smells of German biscuits (cinnamon and nutmeg) and chocolate. Sometimes she gives me a biscuit or a sweetie as a special treat. There are other treasures, kept on the top shelf, which I am allowed to examine. I'm fascinated by the blonde plait wrapped in tissue paper in a box. It's Ulla's hair from when she was a girl, transformed into a woman, her hair cut into a sensible bob.

I examine the photographs on Ulla's mantelpiece.

'Who's this?'

It is a faded group of severe-looking women in long, high-necked dresses.

'My aunts.'

Another photograph of some young women in Charleston dresses.

'Which one are you, Ulla?'

Ulla smiles secretly.

'Who's this?' I point to a young man in an army uniform.

'My brother, Eberhardt. I could only write a few short words to him during the war. The Red Cross got the letters through. He lives in Berlin now, with our ailing mother.'

Without realizing it, German, the second language of Summerhill, becomes as familiar to me as Anna's nagging cough and Ulla's 'Fucking *Scheissmops*', as her wooden Scholl sandals clomp on the bare floorboards. I never learn to speak it, only numbers, and then in two's, which I learn from hearing Ulla counting her knitting, all the way to a hundred. But when I do count, I'm fluent, free from hesitancy. It's not an ordeal. Here my tongue obeys me perhaps because Ulla is kind. We beg hot water at night from her because she has her own kettle. If she declines, I fill my hotty with water from a tepid hot water tap in the freezing cold bathroom.

My French lessons with Ulla don't last long. Someone comes to inspect the school and Ulla, who has no teaching qualifications, is banned from teaching. French and Spanish is now taught by Bill who's from Sunderland, but sounds as foreign as Neill to me. Bill is an elegant man in his late twenties and seems ancient. He's better at teaching French than Ulla, although I miss the little line drawings of Linette and Minette.

Bill doesn't use books. There's a blackboard where he writes things out, but there are no desks, and no flag, just a big wooden table that we all sit around. Mostly we play shops and cafés. My friend Adam is the waiter:

'*Qu'est que vous voulez, mademoiselle?*'

'*Un café, s'il vous plait.*'

'*Café noir ou café au lait?*'

'*Café aux lait, s'il vous plait.*'

There are parcels too, wrapped in greaseproof paper that represent things you can buy in a shop: *du beurre, confiture, sucre.*

I try all the subjects I liked at school in America. I love English where we read stories, and geography where we get to colour in maps. Then there's history with Oliver Bear, fresh from Oxbridge, thick set with impeccable pronunciation, reddish blond hair and a camel duffel coat. We draw maps with our war-requisitioned biros, colouring in delineations of Europe as it once was. And then there are all the kings and queens of England to remember. It's a bit like remembering all the presidents. Oliver throws in a bit of *amo amas amat,* for fun.

At Summerhill, my stammer is never considered a handicap – I am never required to speak unless I feel like it. Our lessons are so intimate – a few of us sitting around a table, that I usually manage to join in a debate – or to give the right answer to something, when I know it. I even manage somehow to say things in meetings; people are patient, no one sniggers or teases me.

Eleanor has been to a maths class, and says I'll like it. She's a bit of a boffin. The class is taught by Neill. We are all curious. Vicky comes along too and she hates maths as much as I do.

We sit around a rickety table in one of the wooden huts. There are seven of us, including my brother Sean, and Neill begins with a joke:

'Maths is really quite simple, even Biscuit, my dog, can count.'

(He's got our interest.)

'I said to him, "Biscuit, how much is two minus two?", and he said nothing!'

We all collectively sigh, our mock exasperation mingled with disappointment. Some of us, like Evie, have heard the joke a hundred times before.

'All right, this is our first algebra class so I'll begin by saying that in algebra we deal with letters instead of numbers. Is that clear? For example (he goes to the blackboard and writes, chalk making a harsh sound against the black):

$a + a = 2a$

$b + b = 2b$

$3a + 6a = 9a$

Now, how much is four people and three horses?'

Vicky: 'There isn't any Neill. You can't add people and horses. It's the same thing as adding apples and oranges.'

Sean: 'Hey, does anybody have an apple? I'm hungry!'

Neill: 'All right, there. Shut up. Good, good, so then, since you can't add apples to oranges, you can't add an a to a b.'

Clancy: 'Hey, can we try?'

Neill: 'Oh, shut up there. All right, try this problem (writing on the blackboard): $4a + 9a + 6a - 3a$.'

Eleanor: 'Here it is Neill. Sixteen a.'

Neill: 'Right.'

Vicky: 'Hey, that's kind of nice and easy, isn't it?'

Neill: 'All right, here's another. See what you do with it: $4a + 3a + 7a - 2a - 5a$."

Vicky: 'Oh, bloody hell, Neill.'

Neill: 'Now come on, it isn't difficult.'

Sean: 'Finished Neill. The answer is seven *a*.'

Neill: 'Right. Try this one: $5a + 6a - 2a - a$'

I was lost at the first hurdle. It's all hieroglyphics to me. Neill sees the increasingly puzzled expression on my face and he tries, impatiently, to explain why the various letters mean numbers and vice versa, but then he stops mid-sentence and tells me, gruffly, using an exaggerated Scots vernacular, to leave.

'Ach away with ye lassie; I've nae time fare the likes of you, you're wasting your time, and mine. Go and find something more interesting to occupy yerself with!'

Even though his gruffness is theatrical, I feel admonished, chastised. He might as well have slapped me. I know he means it and I get out as fast as I can. My face feels flushed from embarrassment, rejection. I wonder what my parents would think if they knew that this would be the last time I will ever, in my entire life, attend a maths lesson.

'Oh shut up and go to sleep.'

Vicky is irritated by my fussing and turning in the bed. Terrified of the dark, I'm going through the nightly ritual of tucking my twenty stuffed animals under the top blanket knitted for me by Grandma Mimmy. It's in purple rainbow wool with a crocheted border.

I have a litany of prayers to go through before I can go to sleep. I save the most important one, 'Now I Lay Me Down to Sleep', until last. It's my insurance policy. It finishes with, 'If I should die before I wake, I pray the Lord my soul to take,' and I cross myself at the end, just to make sure.

'Evie, please …' I plead.

Evie is the most obliging, kindly letting me get into the bunk with her, opening her blanket to let me in. My own bed is over-crowded and I'm not proud. It'll be an uncomfortable sleep, but the warmth of someone next to me, however grumpy they might be, is preferable to feeling alone and afraid.

Sometimes I scamper along the corridor and slip into bed with my little brother, but he is a chaotic sleeper, flailing about and muttering in his sleep.

Lying in bed, unable to sleep, I have imaginary conversations with my sister. I want to talk about Mom's funeral, about her dress and the roses covering her feet. I wonder if she was wearing shoes? If she was, they would be her favourite ones – the shiny black stilet-tos – to match her favourite black dress, the one with three-quarter length sleeves. Deedee will bring up the subject of the buffet pre-pared by Corwith's Pharmacy on Main Street and how delicious the chicken salad sandwiches were.

'I was waiting outside the white Presbyterian Church on the corner of Main Street after my piano lesson,' I tell Deedee, piecing together events. 'Mom should've been driving from the east end of the Island to pick me up.'

'Then I came running towards you down Main Street,' says Deedee.

I stop talking.

I am watching Deedee's steady progress. She's out of breath by the time she reaches the edge of the sidewalk, across the road from where I'm standing.

'Mom's had an accident,' she shouts.

'Ha, ha, very funny.'

Then I realize Deedee isn't joking. Tears are running down her face as she arrives by my side, and takes my hand.

After the accident we drive home with Mimmy in her maroon-coloured car known as 'The Kaiser'.

Mimmy has been living with us for a while in a room, or 'quarters', at the side of the house, by the back door. She has a big cabinet in polished veneer, a bed with a hand-knitted bedspread, and cooking facilities of some kind. She makes me little dishes of rice pudding, which I love.

Twice, she's taken Deedee and Bob to Disneyland, driving them west across the desert, stopping every evening at a motel with a kidney-shaped swimming pool. The car has a kind of primitive air-conditioning. You put ice cubes in a little contraption and pull a string, making a fan go round and round, circulating ice-cube air.

Right now my sister is sitting in the front, next to Mimmy. I am alone in the back.

Deedee: 'Is Mom going to be all right?'

Mimmy clears her throat. 'Well dear, your mother's last words to me at the hospital were, "Take care of my babies."'

And then I hear huge, grown-up sobs, coming not from my

grandmother, but from my sister – not the cries of a child, but serious, adult sobbing.

I think Mom must be dead. But I'm still not sure. Mimmy hasn't said so exactly, but my sister's sobbing seems to tell me that's what's happened. Mimmy carries on driving.

Later, when my stepfather tells us that our mother never regained consciousness before she slipped away, I wonder if Mimmy was telling the truth about Mom's last words. Perhaps she was telling a 'white lie' to soften the blow, or maybe she wants to stake her claim, like they do in a gold rush, because she knows her days living with us are numbered, as she doesn't get on with my stepfather. Maybe it's my stepfather who's telling the white lie. But the truth is, Mom's dead, that's for certain.

Ulla runs the sewing classes, two till five, every afternoon from her patchwork-quilted, rag-rugged bedroom. A new rug is woven every year from a new set of rags.

I learn about Ulla's sewing classes by accident.

'I like your nightgown,' I tell Evie.

It's a flannel nightgown, pale pink with dark pink flowers scattered over it, frilly cuffs, and mother of pearl buttons down the front bodice, or yoke.

'Thanks. I made it.'

'How?'

'In Ulla's room.'

'D'you think I could make one?'

'Yeah, I'm sure Ulla would show you. Come to her sewing class after lunch.'

I arrive at two.

'We will start with an apron,' says Ulla.

The first thing Ulla does is to teach me how to thread a needle. 'Don't make the thread too long or it will tangle up.'

Then she shows me how to make a knot at the end of the thread. This is most important thing. She holds the needle in her right hand, and winds the end of the thread a few times around it, pulls it through, and hey presto, a perfect knot every time.

'Here. For you.'

She gives me a length of gingham and shows me how to sew two lines of running stitch along the top, and later, coaxing the stitches into gathers, onto a long, narrow strip of fabric for the waistband and ties. The little squares in the fabric are useful and help me keep my stitches straight and even. She cuts out a square of fabric for a pocket, which I attach to the side of the apron. Then she teaches me how to embroider a row of decorative cross-stitching along the hem.

Ulla's classes are run with military precision. Bad boys are put to work, cutting stuffing up for the stuffing box (it doubles as a seat), taking their destructive urges out on the fabric. At the end of the lesson, 5 p.m. precisely, everyone has to tidy up and put things away in their places in the cupboards. Someone is given the magnet. I like this job. You have to run it over the floorboards, picking up any stray pins, and put them into a little wooden bowl.

Everything has a place; everything has a method. Good work is rewarded. Bad work is unpicked and you have to begin again. Sometimes the sewing fairy intervenes over night and sorts it all out for you. I finish my gingham apron, cross-stitched at the hem, with Ulla praising my handiwork. I graduate to the flannel nightgown (this takes almost a term) and then on to extravagant dresses, made from curtain material, and then a tailored Harris Tweed maxi-coat.

We make stuffed animals from a selection of coloured felt. I make a fox hand-puppet, in brown and white felt, with thread for whiskers, which are a bit too floppy. Instead of buttons, I can have glass eyes because I've sewn him so well. There is even a loom where you can weave bags; you can make pillow lace, and shuttle. If you have the patience, you can knit a Fair Isle jumper or make a pair of leather gloves. Nothing is ruled out.

Sean has a go at knitting a scarf.

'Knit one, purl one,' he mutters beneath his breath.

Knitting is something everyone does, even the boys, when they're sitting in a meeting or just talking in their rooms. I decide to knit a sweater with a Fair Isle pattern across the chest for Uncle Tom. Ulla takes me to the haberdasher's in Leiston to choose my wool. It's called Ariel and the colour is Pine Green. I opt for white, brown and grey for the pattern in the Fair Isle. It takes me all term to finish it. Ulla parcels it up for me, tying it with her precious pieces of string, and sending it off in the Christmas post.

I wonder if it will reach him, in America.

Why did Mom never learn to sew, I wonder, but of course

I'll never know. When I start Brownies, age seven, I need to alter my uniform (a hand-me-down from my sister) so that the dress sits just below the knee. I ask Mom to do it but my request goes unheeded so I take up the hem *myself* with iron-on tape. I'm soon making dresses for my dolls, wrapping and tying fabric onto their plastic bodies. Later I make a fuss about wanting a bride's costume for Halloween, which Mom had promised to buy me and forgotten about. She slaps me across the face. Immediately ashamed, she lets me go trick or treating in her mink stole and a pair of rhinestone earrings with the clips that are too painful to tolerate for any length of time.

With Ulla's help, I swap reading for sewing.

Chapter 5

'La, la, la, la, la, la, la. Me, me, me, me, me, me, me…'

Mom is singing scales at the piano. She starts off impossibly low, pressing a key on the left side of the piano, but as she repeats the scale, moving her finger along the keyboard, her voice gets higher and higher. I wonder how far she can go and whether the windows will shatter like they do in cartoons.

Deedee says Mom met my father at the Stork Club, or maybe Armando's. But Bob says she was acting in summer rep in a little theatre upstate when she met my father. It was opening night and he had an investment in the company. With one eye on Hollywood and the other on the Met, Mom, full name Betsy Ryan, studied drama at the Pasadena Playhouse, and opera somewhere back east, maybe even the Julliard School. They were married within three months and she settled into life on Long Island, with a baby every eighteen months, and the occasional recital or amateur theatrical to keep her hand in.

When she is well, music fills the house. The piano, an upright, is laden with sheet music from the latest musicals, well thumbed: *My Fair Lady* (a drawing on the cover of a man in a top hat, pulling the strings of a lady marionette); *South Pacific* (Mitzi Gaynor stretching her arms up to the blue sky in gay abandon). I know the words to all of the songs.

After my parent's divorce, and the ensuing custody battle – the first of many – we go and live with our father. I'm tormented by my longing for Mom. I wait, bewildered, every day for her to come and get us. The waiting seems endless and the days seem to stretch on for ever. When will she come and get us?

My waiting pays off.

I can see the Packard coming down the long driveway with Mom at the wheel.

'Mom's here! Mom's come to get us!'

My father and Mary have gone to Tennessee for a couple of days to get married, and Violet, my grandmother's African American maid from the South, who came with us to our father's house in Smithtown after the divorce, has been left in charge of us.

'Get your things, children, I'm taking you home with me.'

Mom pulls the bedspread from my bed, and starts piling everything into it, my Raggedy Ann doll with her smile half torn off, my clothes from the chest of drawers and the wardrobe. Then she ties everything into a giant-sized hobo bundle.

'Get your coats, children.'

Vidy is fussing about us. 'Oh, Mrs Cuddihy, what am I going to tell Mr Cuddihy when he gets home?'

'Tell him I forced you at gunpoint and there was nothing you could do to stop me.'

I feel sorry for Vidy, leaving her behind like that, but we pile into Mom's Packard with shouts of, 'Whoopee! This is *so* exciting.'

She takes us to the farmhouse she shares with my stepfather, Larry, where we spend a couple of blissful days and nights. But then we have to hide in a back room with Mimmy, because my father and Mary have come to take us 'home'.

'Shussh, children, quiet,' she says.

My father knocks on the door. There is fighting, grown-ups crying, someone falling down the stairs. Later, my stepfather is seen slumped in an armchair, weeping. I've never seen a grown man cry. Why, only last night he'd been dancing me round the living room on his great big shoes. I love that feeling of being led. He can shout my brothers into silence with his deep man's voice, but now here he is bawling like a baby.

We return to Smithtown with my father, but it doesn't matter how unfit the courts have declared my mother (she's an 'alcoholic' and sometimes lashes out at us), she's my mother and I miss her.

Then Daddy dies.

My stepmother Mary flies us all to her parents in Tennessee. Vidy doesn't come with us. It occurs to me that a lot of people are ill-defined by their names. Take Vidy, for example. Her full name is Violet Lively, but she's slow and languorous, partly due to her arthritis and her age. She's been with Grandma since my father was a child. I only once see her move swiftly, when the cat jumps onto the table and licks the butter.

Then there's my stepmother Mary Smiley. I never once see her smile. My uncles refer to her privately as The Unsmiling Miss Smiley, otherwise known as my 'wicked stepmother'. Mary, who gave my naughty brothers cold showers when they misbehaved and even smacked my open palms with a ruler when I was bad, was at her best when she was making clothes for my sister and myself. Often the outfits were matching, in different sizes. My sister sneered at the dresses for not being store-bought, or even, when we were very wealthy, delivered to the door by the man from Rowes of Bond Street. I secretly found them rather exotic. It seemed like magic, the way she could transform a piece of fabric into a beautiful dress.

Mary only tolerates Vidy because of my father, and vice versa, I suspect, so Vidy is sent back to my Grandmother in Park Avenue, heartbroken after my father's death. She leaves in a taxi, her gloved hand waving a gentle goodbye from the back window.

Chrissy and I race after the car: 'Goodbye Vidy, goodbye…'

Grandma and Grandpa Smiley live on the outskirts of Knoxville with enough land to keep chickens (which peck my fingers when I help Grandma S feed them), and they grow their own vegetables. It's my first time in an airplane. We fly through thunder and lighting. I'm terrified but my brothers laugh defiantly, as if they are on a fairground ride.

The Smileys look like the Waltons. Grandma S never seems to

take off her apron and Grandpa S wears denim overalls, except when he goes into Knoxville where he works as a projectionist in the movie theatre. Then he changes into a sports jacket and bow tie.

We spend the summer there.

One day we all pile into his Ford pick-up to go and see *The Incredible Shrinking Man*. I feel desperately worried for the shrinking man. His shouts for attention go unnoticed by his grieving wife as she locks their house up and walks away from him, for ever.

'Don't leave him!' I want to shout. *Go back.*

We play in an abandoned house near the Smileys. My sister spends a lot of the time outside, her bare feet prickled by the hard bleached grass, practising being a majorette with a cheerleader's baton she has found in one of the rooms. Indoors there is a black, stand up Bakelite telephone with a big clunky dial.

I call Mom. 'Hi Mommy, it's Mikey, You can come and get us now.'

I make up Mom's questions, listening to the blankness on the other end of the imaginary line.

'We're fine, Mommy, but I wanted to know when are you going to come and get us. I miss you, Mommy.'

All the crockery is there in the kitchen, everything in place as if it has just been left, but there are no grown-ups to boss us around.

We play kitchens, and I cook all the meals I remember my mother preparing for us, spaghetti sauce, apple pie and I pretend to roll out the pastry. My little brother is willing to enter into the game and eats everything I cook for him.

Mary has obviously learnt her discipline techniques from her parents and although my sister and I manage to avoid being hit by Grandma and Grandpa Smiley, Grandpa S whips Sean with a belt for persuading me to bite into a chilli pepper he has picked in the pepper patch. As soon as I bite into it, the shocking heat of it burns my tongue, and my mouth feels as if it's on fire. I cry loudly and melodramatically. Afterwards, I feel ashamed for making such a fuss, alarmed that Sean is taking such a beating from this soft-spoken old man, and it's my fault.

Sean flails about, trying to run away, but the old man seems to have super-human strength, holding Sean with one hand, and beating him with the other. I guess he's had a lot of practice.

In November, there is another custody battle in the courts. The newspapers carry the story with a photograph of Mary, a headshot, wearing a small white hat just covering the top of her blonde, chignoned head, the stiff net casting a glamorous veil across her eyes, with her lips immaculately coloured in to illustrate the head-line: PUBLISHING HEIR'S WIDOW TELLS COURT OF HUSBAND'S DYING WISH.

Apparently our father had whispered, 'Take care of the kids, Mary,' before he expired.

This isn't enough to convince the judge. Our mother, by the time things have come to court, has cleaned up her act, married our stepfather and had a baby. She gives a convincing performance and the judge grants her custody. We are returned, triumphantly, to our mother and we move into a freshly painted farmhouse, just outside

Southampton, with Mom's new baby, our little sister, Nanette. The house is painted pale yellow, surrounded by lilac bushes, which burst into bloom the following summer. I share a room with my big sister, Deedee. I am thrilled with the room and the opportunity to share with my sister, but she resents the downsizing from our Smithtown mansion to a five-bedroom farmhouse; sharing a room with her little sister is not on her list of priorities.

We have new blankets. Mine is pale pink, edged with a thick strip of satin at the top and bottom with darker pink roses printed into the fabric. Deedee's blanket is blue, with the same, darker roses scattered across the surface. There is a fancy white dressing table with three mirrors on it, so you can see your face in profile, and a curvy glass jar, waving in and out, a pink ribbon tied around it, filled with multicoloured sweets. It all seems so perfect.

I wake up in the middle of the night. My face feels taut and sticky and there is a horrible chemical smell. My sister is standing over me, laughing, holding a bottle of nail varnish in her hand. She has been painting my face with it. Mom is too sleepy to get up and sort it out, so my sister scrubs it off with a toothbrush.

Sometimes when I wake in the middle of the night desperate for a cuddle, Mom's not there (either drying out or on a bender), and in her place is a fat Polish lady in a white maid's uniform.

'I'm scared,' I bleat into the darkness.

Otherwise I become Deedee and Bob's stooge. My sister is shaking me awake: 'Get up, it's time to get ready for school, you'll be late.'

Dressed and downstairs eating my cornflakes, I sense that something isn't quite right.

'Gee, it's awfully dark outside.'

Their sniggers erupt into mocking laughter, because of course it's the middle of the night.

Sometimes the joke's on Mom as she lies passed out on her bed, either drunk or on sleeping pills. One night my brother Sean puts a lighted cigarette between Mom's fingers. She sleeps on, oblivious.

One weekend my mother and stepfather go away to a realtor's convention. Uncle Gordon, our current lodger who my mother met at an AA meeting (he's an artist who sports a beret and a grey goatee beard, as if to prove the point), turns our front lawn into a miniature golf course. A keen golfer, he transforms it with sandpits and poles with little flags on them.

My mother has given Gordon money to buy food for us five children (my older brother Bob is away by this time at boarding school). But Gordon goes on a bender, hence the grass soup he prepares, which none of us eat. We make do with cornflakes and water and then go to the neighbours for help.

Chapter 6

Tuesday evening, November 1962: Neill is trying to address the issue of swearing. (Believe it or not, fuck, shit, bugger, cunt gets boring after a while.) He's gathered a group of older kids in the staff room, which is cosier than the lounge. There is a fire burning in the grate. Biscuit is curled up at his feet. The older kids present consist of Pete Love, a blond, lanky bespectacled American, Holly, Pete's sparring partner, with long silky hair and a soft, slightly Cockney accent, and Zoë, Neill's sixteen-year-old daughter, tall, with short, dark hair who speaks with confidence and self-assurance. Then there's Kat, Vicky's bossy, outspoken older sister, and Nicky, a budding rock and roll guitarist, always clad in a sheepskin jacket.

We younger and less vocal ones look on from the sidelines, silent.

Neill: 'I've got you all together here tonight, because there seems to be a lot of swearing going on in the school, more than usual. I want to know why this is happening, and whether you think it's appropriate to use language that people outside our community might find offensive.'

Pete: 'A lot of new kids have arrived this term who've been brought up to think swearing is taboo, so they're just letting rip.'

Holly: 'They like swearing; it just works for them.'

Zoë: 'It can also be used in an affectionate way, Neill. Calling someone an old bastard could be a term of endearment.'

Neill puffs on his pipe: Humph.

He goes on: 'I wonder if you've ever thought of the wider implications of swearing? Whether this could endanger the school? We're all used to it here, but what happens if a relative comes to visit the school; say they've paid the fees for that child, and the first word they hear is a swear word. Will they be impressed? I don't think so, and it's very possible that they could withdraw the child from the school. So, do you think it's worth the risk? To lose a child from Summerhill because of swearing?'

Holly: 'Look, Neill, the kids who are swearing don't think the words they're using are bad. It's the people who come here who have the dirty minds.'

Zoë: 'Are we having a discussion or are you trying to get us to stop swearing, Neill?'

Neill: 'You know I can't stop you from swearing. I just wanted to talk about it.'

Pete: 'If a visitor takes their child away because he's offended by a bit of swearing, then he was probably looking for an excuse.'

Kat: 'You might as well have us all wearing uniforms, blazers and ties, with the girls in pleated skirts. Maybe the visitors would like that!'

Neill: 'I'll have you know that very recently someone from the town said that the bad language used by Summerhill children was a danger to the nice children of Leiston.'

Nicky: 'Neill, if you think we're bad, you should listen to the downtown kids at the cinema. Their swearing is much worse than ours.'

Neill: 'Look, it's not a question of morality, it's a question of finances. Am I going to lose pupils because of swearing? That's the point I'm trying to make.'

Olly: 'Oh come on Neill, when did you last lose a pupil because of swearing?'

Neill: 'Well, there was one man, I remember…'

Olly: 'One man in over forty years, Neill?'

(Laughter)

Neill: '… came to the school to see his kid, and heard things that didn't please him, so he put his kid in the car, and drove off. I was rather pleased in a way. I never gave him back his fees.'

Everyone laughs, and Neill looks at his watch.

Neill: 'Well, that seems like a good place to finish this discussion.'

And he lifts himself out of the chair, with some difficulty, eases himself into his overcoat, and off he goes.

I think about Mom and I wonder if Neill knows that 'fucking bastard' is the most beautiful thing in the world?

'Come on,' the shout goes up.

It's Wednesday evening and Ena is bringing her country dancing LPs over from her cottage. We are terrified of Ena.

Ena is Neill's second wife. She is twenty-five years younger than him, short and square and mostly bosom with black gypsy hair, always braided and wrapped around her head. Gold earrings dangle from her pierced ears (unusual for those times). She wears cotton shifts, sleeveless, with a cardigan wrapped over her shoulders in cold weather, and sheer stockings, always slightly twisted at the ankles. She runs all the practical, day to day aspects of the school with a rod of iron.

She can freeze a room of rowdy children with: 'Listen, you lot!' Besides the General Meeting, there are only two organized activities at Summerhill, Spontaneous Acting led by Neill on Sunday evenings, and Ena's Country Dancing, which takes place on Wednesdays.

She's standing in the gram box, a raised platform boxed in at two sides, in the right hand far corner of the lounge. You climb up the ladder attached to the side of it to find a turntable and piles and piles of records, spanning the last twenty years: Del Shannon's 'Three Steps to Heaven', the Beatles, the Rolling Stones, the Kinks, Elvis. Speakers are wired in at two corners of the room to form a kind of makeshift stereo. The ceiling above her is graffitied with the names of singers, some of them well past their sell-by date. CLIFF in fuzzy black letters, burnt on with match smoke, and SINATRA less noticeable, scratched on with a penknife.

Ena conducts proceedings from on high, pointing to the rabble of beatnik children below: 'OK, grab your partner, and forward, two, three, four, five, six, seven, eight. And back, two, three, four, five, six, seven, eight. *Pas de bas*, and turn. Figure of eight. Line of three, I said *three*, and forward. And forward, under and over. Here we go, once again. Two, three, four, five, six, seven, eight. Line of three, *pas de bas. Pas de bas*, Mikey.'

We love Ena's country dancing sessions, and learn all the moves to The Eightsome Reel and Strip the Willow as Ena shouts instructions from her vantage point. My favourite is the Gay Gordons where you loop and walk backwards and forwards, twirling your partner in different ways. I'm tall and have to be a boy because there are more girls who are willing to be ordered about on the floor, than there are boys.

As an adult, I will find it difficult to be lead by a man.

I am always hungry. If the food is halfway decent that day, we are reduced to begging for seconds while cringing in anticipation of a shouted rebuff. Being shouted at by Ena is the next worst thing to a clip around the ear. And Lord save us if we should complain the milk's off, which it often is. It arrives every morning in huge metal milk churns, which are rocked into the kitchen, and ladled into metal jugs. I'd love to be allowed in the kitchen, but it's strictly out of bounds. Children are excluded. No argument. Ena is boss.

I long for the luxury of toast. Thick white cotton wool slices, oozing melted butter. Neill has wholemeal bread made to a 'special recipe' at the bakery in town. There is a pile of it every morning, stacked on a cracked platter in the dining room, spread with margarine. If the bread isn't mouldy, we save it for later, scraping the margarine off, toasting it on an older kid's electric fire, and re-applying the margarine. We save our breaktime milk too (the little third of a pint bottles that Mrs Thatcher Milk Snatcher took away when she was Education Secretary), and heat it up on a banned methylated spirit stove, flavouring it with Camp coffee essence. Sometimes, more luxuriously, someone might have a little tin of Nescafé with the skin of aluminium sealing it. When you punch it through, you get a lovely whiff of coffee granules.

I'm not sure if it's to feel closer to Mom or the opportunity to dress up in a fake fur jacket, lent by my best friend Vicky, that I decide to attend the Catholic Church in the local town on Sundays. I put on a dress for the first and only time that week and go on my own.

It doesn't seem so long ago that I'm dressed in a beautiful, frothy white dress, white shoes and socks, and a veil at my First Holy Communion. I look just like a bride. Best of all, Grandma Cuddihy has given me a new white prayer book with the edges of each page dipped in gold, so that when it's closed it looks like the side of the book is one thick block of pure gold. Sister John presents me with a new, white rosary as well.

The church in Leiston reminds me of our church back home. There is even a crucified Christ at the front, sheltered by his own little wooden roof, and a statue of the Virgin Mary. The familiar smell of incense, the Latin prayers, the liturgies; the Our Fathers and Hail Marys bring me closer to the past than I have felt in months.

Neill is rather bemused by my Catholicism. In his atheist idyll, religion is seen as an act of rebellion. I light a candle for my mother and return to school feeling I've done something rather dramatic and noble.

A few weeks later, Neill calls me into his office for a 'PL'. Neill conducts this so-called Private Lesson as more of a psychotherapy session than a ticking off or sermon, although I don't recognize it at the time. A PL is an honour he bestows on anyone who looks like they need special attention.

We see Neill as a kindly grandfather figure. Despite his unconventional attitudes to education, Neill is from another century. He's a Victorian, born in 1883. (I picture long dresses, men in stiff high collared shirts, horse-drawn carriages.) He puffs on his pipe, which always seems to be going out and asks, 'Are ye still a Catholic?'

'Well, I say my prayers before I go to sleep at night. But I haven't been to church for ages.'

'I see. And how do you feel about that?'

'You mean not going to church?'

'Aye. Do you feel guilty?'

'Kind of… I ggguess so.'

'And do you feel guilty about other things?'

'What other things?'

'You tell me.'

'Well, Vicky and I teased Bonnie. We made up a song about her and made her cry. I feel guilty about that.'

'I see. Anything else?'

I'm beginning to feel like I'm at confession, telling the priest I said shut up three times and darn once.

There is a long silence. The smoke between us has got thicker. Someone knocks on the door. Neill is wanted for something or other.

'Aye, that'll be all,' he releases me from the inquisition.

The next time I bump into him, he asks the same question: 'Are you still a Catholic?'

I laugh. 'Maybe.'

I sense it's become a bit of a running joke, which is Neill's way of saying he doesn't approve. Anyway, I don't go to church for long. Buttered toast at Tufford's café on Sunday mornings offers me more comfort than a cold host, dipped in communion wine.

Chapter 7

Our first Christmas in England arrives and with it, a huge parcel from America made up by my Aunt Joan. Inside are little portable tape-recorders for my younger brother and myself, a teddy-bear pyjama case for me. There are presents from Grandma Cuddihy. Mine is wrapped in a slim, Saks Fifth Avenue gift box covered in gold paper, patterned with white snowflake doilies, and clever, red, elasticized ribbon tied around it. Inside (lined a cheerful red) lie three pairs of stockings, American tan, delicately interleaved with tissue paper. I am both thrilled and disappointed. The stockings are for a woman. I am ten years old, still a child, running wild in patched jeans and sneakers, and I have no use for them, but the thought that I might some day wear them is intriguing.

What I want more than anything is a Spanish costume doll, which I covet, passing a shop in Notting Hill.

I've been invited to stay with Evie and her mother Myrtle who live in Bohemian splendour in a ground floor flat in London. Over the years, Myrtle will keep an open house of musicians, actors and ex-Summerhillians, including my little brother.

When I first set eyes on the house, painted an improbable shade of fairytale pink, with its huge crumbling pillars and portico, I think the whole building is theirs. When we step inside, there is a long corridor, with a door at the end of it, which Myrtle unlocks with another key. This is where she lives.

The flat is partitioned with inadequate plywood walls, which make the rooms disproportionately high and narrow. Fancy cornicing is blocked off in mid-sequence by an abrupt corner. The windows don't realize their true potential grandeur. Evie's Aunt Maggie, an actress who often appears as an extra on *Coronation Street* shares the flat. She sleeps on the other side of the wall from Evie. Evie's side is latticed with 2 x 1, like the back of a stage set. Evie is saving egg boxes to make her room soundproof. She has covered half the room already. She will often return to school after the holidays with purple shadows under her eyes from all the late nights. I think she welcomes the comparative orderliness of school with its bedtimes and lights out by 10 p.m.

Notting Hill looks like a winter wonderland, with all the dereliction from the war, the bomb sites edged with corrugated iron, covered prettily in a deep layer of snow.

Evie's father takes us out to Kensington Gardens where we watch the skaters on the Round Pond, which is unusually deeply frozen. It is beautiful like an enchanted fairyland. He takes us to somewhere called Harrods, which turns out to be an enormous department store, and tells us to choose a present, anything we like.

I choose a sewing basket, white and blue lacquered straw, lined in quilted sky blue satin, with compartments.

For the end of term party, before the Christmas break, Ena had presented me with a red satin dress with a matching sash lined in white; she'd made the dress for her daughter, Zoë – now a gangly teenager – some years before. With its puffy sleeves and full skirt, it seems a little old-fashioned, a little babyish for a five-foot-two ten-year-old but I love the petticoat that comes with it. It's made from white net and punctuated with embroidered roses, like flat strawberries. I stammer my thanks but it is now that I decide, once and for all, that I will be better off making my own things. The sewing basket will help me do this.

I never stop wishing for that Spanish doll.

At Evie's home, I am treated with kindness but I know instinctively that I have to be on my best behaviour. Withdrawn and stammering, I'm not the most glorious child to have around. It feels odd, watching strangers opening their presents away from my siblings, and their familiar banter. I wonder what Bob, Deedee, Sean and Chrissy are up to?

Locked in the loo, I bring out my treasured photo album given to me by Mimmy, with its shiny green cover. The photos were taken with a Polaroid land camera. Larry would take a photo, time it for sixty seconds with his watch, pull out the photo and the paper seal from the back, and we would watch the image appear, with it's frilly border, as if by magic. Then he would rub a lipstick-sized stick of fixative over the front that smelled of chemicals, to fix the image forever.

My favourite photo is the Christmas one taken at the farmhouse. Mommy is putting the finishing touches to the tree, decorating it with angel hair, hanging from its branches. She is wearing her quilted dressing gown and her shiny black stilettos, squatting, reaching under the tree, and arranging presents. Her dark, shoulder-length hair is the same length as mine is now. In the foreground sits a big box with a cellophane front.

Is that the doll I got for Christmas or my sister's Deedee's Queen Alexandra doll?

I'll never know. What I do know is that to the left, just out of camera shot, is the mantelpiece with our stockings hung expectantly, one for Patsy the dog as well.

On the back of the photo in Larry's fine American script, it reads: *Finishing touches, Xmas '57.*

It must be our first Christmas back with Mom and Larry after my father died, and the judge had granted Mom custody. Everything was all right again, just for a short while.

With the Big Freeze of 1962 comes snow right through until the following February. It's so cold that the empty fireplace in the library is filled with coal, and stays alight all day. I find a copy of *The Lion, the Witch and the Wardrobe* by C. S. Lewis. Peter, Susan and their two younger siblings, who are evacuated to a big house in the countryside during the war, also have to live with their absent-minded uncle. The magical land they discover at the back of the wardrobe, the talking animals, the arguments, the betrayals and reconciliations between the siblings – it all makes sense to me. And all that snow, the dead coming back to life. I'm transported, hooked, and I read every volume.

Although I'm mostly too shy to join in, I love being around Neill when he directs Spontaneous Acting. The lounge fills up with children, making it the perfect place to stay warm.

'Now, let's see, I'm St Peter at the gates of heaven. You've died, and have come to the gates, and want to get in – any volunteers?'

Spontaneous Acting is our opportunity to interact with Neill, to be clever and admired. Neill sits there puffing on his pipe. The rest of us sit cross-legged on the floor, looking up at him. Hands plunge wildly skyward as everyone vies for a chance to show off.

Neill points to Sean, who gets up and strides across the room to Neill. Back in America, Sean played the prince in a school production of Oscar Wilde's *The Happy Prince*. The prince has jewels for eyes, which he generously offers to a sparrow to feed the poor of the parish. After that he's blind. He doesn't want to see the misery and poverty around him so he doesn't miss his sight.

'That's my brother the Prince up there on the stage!' I told everyone around me.

I was so proud of my brother.

Sean looks up at Neill. 'Hello. Are you St Peter?'

Neill: 'Yes, yes, I think so.'

Sean: 'Well, um, I'm trying to get into heaven. Which way is it?'

Neill: 'It doesn't make any difference. What sort of person are you?'

Sean: 'Well, I'm a fabulous person actually. I've only told around a thousand lies, and I've only killed a few people.'

Neill: 'You expect to go to heaven after all that?'

Sean: 'Of course, why not?'

Neill: 'Well, that's rather original. Maybe you'll help some of them in here. OK, this way.'

Adam is next. (He comes up to Neill snapping a camera.) 'Say, could you tell me about your second divorce? You are St Peter, aren't you? Well, good. Now, I'm from the *Daily Blab*, and our paper wants to do a feature on you. Now, could you tell us a little about yourself?'

Neill: 'No, I'm not a very big guy. I only keep the golden key.'

Adam: 'How much is it worth?'

Neill: 'You've been educated in America, I see.'

Adam: 'Obviously. Can I see the key?'

Neill: 'Oh, no! I never give it up.'

Adam: 'Well, then, a picture.'

Neill: 'Get out of here. I don't want you here!'

Adam: 'Well, if that's your attitude, keep your old clouds.'

Neill: 'OK. Now I'm going to be a governor of a prison. You've had a few years in prison, and so when you are set free you have to go to the governor's office, and he talks to you before you leave. Now, who will be the first criminal?'

Chapter 8

Ulla saves string. She is in charge of the post and takes the parcels she has tied up with clever knots, using salvaged bits of string, to the post office every day. Bill is in charge of the chickens and three bossy geese. Olly directs the end of term plays, and Judith – an overweight, greasy-haired woman with pointy glasses – well, she seems to have come as a job lot with her husband, Adrian, who teaches woodwork. Adrian is Jack Spratt, a lean, bearded, well-spoken Englishman with an energy Judith doesn't possess. They are opposites. He light and quick, she dark, slow and glum. Judith teaches English to Chrissy's age group, and is housemother to some of the younger children. She keeps a beady but unenthusiastic eye on her charges.

At dinnertime I see Judith sitting next to Chrissy who is wriggling.

'Get off.' He swots her hands away like a pesky fly.

Later on, I go to find Chrissy but I can't find him anywhere. I end up in the pottery shed, which has the same status as Ulla's room. Sure enough, Chrissy is chatting to Myles, Ena's 35-year-old son by her first marriage. Myles has been taught by a world-famous potter called Bernard Leach, a British potter who studied in Japan, and everyone wants to be Myles's friend. The pottery shed is the best-equipped classroom in the school with two wheels and a kiln firing pots on a regular basis. Myles can magic a pot from a lump of slimy clay, spinning round and round, hypnotically on the wheel.

He persuades Chrissy to have a go. Chrissy's hands are a little small, but he manages to centre his lump of clay and make something that passes for a pot, first time round. It's better than I can manage. I can't even centre my piece of clay, it spins wildly out of control, and I give up. Instead, I make a box from slabs of clay that Myles rolls out, with a narrow rolling pin, like very thick, grey pastry.

'Hey Chrissy, do you want to come to Ulla's room?' I ask but he shakes his head and I retreat on my own.

'Now you lot, we must get a move on.'

We are knitting squares for a blanket that is to be given to Neill for his eightieth birthday. We are gathered in Ulla's room, which is warm, making it perfect for socializing. Everyone is contributing to the blanket, even little kids who can barely master their knitting needles and constantly drop their stitches with Ulla tut-tutting as she rescues a grubby rag of knitting for the umpteenth time. Adept knitters make elaborate squares with Arran plaits in them. Fast knitters like Evie make several squares to add to the paltry and misshapen pile gathering in the basket in Ulla's room. It's going to be an interesting blanket.

'*Ach mensch.*'

Ulla's expressions of exasperation are always in German.

'*Du hast einen Vogel.*'

Or sometimes English: 'Do not teach your granny to suck eggs.'

And more prosaically when she's trying to cheer me up: 'One swallow does not a summer make.' (I'm not sure what this means, but it sounds like something to do with food.)

Sometimes, Ulla makes sexual innuendos, which seem beneath her. Sewing poppers onto an item of clothing, she demonstrates in a silly voice: '*Naja*, this is the man (the bit of popper that sticks out) and we put him into the hole in the "lady" popper like so.'

And she laughs with her mouth opened in a silly wide grin, her glasses balanced at the end of her nose.

I roll my eyes in disgust.

Bickering has broken out between two of the older girls. Laura, recently arrived from America, is in disagreement with Marla Feinberg about her piece of knitting. Marla says it looks like shit. Laura loses it and grabs a knitting needle. Lifting it high, aiming very precisely, she stabs Marla in the thigh.

'You're revolting, revolting, revolting!' she shouts.

Almost immediately, three beads of blood appear on Marla's plump jeaned thigh.

We gasp.

Up until now, I've witnessed a bit of arm punching, kids play wrestling on the floor, that kind of thing. This is violent, serious.

Ulla ushers us out, for once calm.

'Now, off you go everyone, I will sort this out. Vicky, go and see if Laura is all right. Marla, you stay here. Don't cry, it's not so bad. I will clean the wound. Adam, can you fetch me some cotton wool from the cupboard. Thank you. Now off you go everyone…'

We are stunned. Silent. Laura has had outbursts before but nothing like this. The incident is discussed in the meeting. Laura is absent, ashamed and angry. There is no fine or punishment. Soon word reaches us that Neill has asked her to leave.

Sean hates Summerhill. There are no sports for him to excel at, so he spends a lot of time annoying other kids, or downtown. Sometimes he runs away, letting me in on his secret later on, tearfully, but he always comes back; he has a terrible sense of direction and besides, where would he go? I never see him during the day. He spends most of his time playing the pinball machines in the local café (he is good at numbers) where he befriends the owner. Eventually Leslie, the café owner, gives him a job peeling potatoes in return for egg and chips at lunchtimes. Wearing his jacket with the Southampton Mariners logo stitched across the back, he watches the local football team, playing their game, wishing he had a team to play with.

Then Sean tries to run away *properly*. He persuades Chrissy to go with him. The older boys, Clancy, Pete, Jim Darling and a few others, chase them around town carrying sticks and cricket bats in case Sean gets violent. They catch up with them on the railway footbridge and bring them back to the school.

On Saturday evening, after dinner, the weekly General Meeting takes place. It follows the Friday afternoon Tribunal where rule-breakers are brought to justice and fined. The great hall or lounge, as we call it, is a cavernous space with huge fireplaces (never lit) at either end, and two sets of dilapidated French windows, which once looked out onto magnificent gardens, and now look out to mud-patched grass, some swings and a see-saw. There is no furniture, just bare floorboards, which we sit on, cross-legged. Twice a week, cheerful ladies from the town push their mops around the floor, the dirty grey strings dragging liquid wax the colour of snot.

Anyone who has a suggestion or a new law to propose (to add to the several already) can bring it up. At the beginning of every term, a chairman is elected, usually an older kid, for one meeting only. At the end of the meeting, he chooses another kid as his successor.

Certain offences carry automatic fines:

- Riding another person's bike without permission: an automatic fine of sixpence
- Swearing in town (you can swear as much as you like in the school grounds)
- Bad behaviour in the cinema
- Climbing on roofs
- Throwing food in the dining room.

Punishments are nearly always fines: hand over pocket money for a week or miss a cinema night.

The report from the Friday Tribunal is read out on Saturday night, then the Agenda. After that, it's AOB (any other business). The chairman stands, leaning against a wooden mantelpiece, with Neill sat facing him or her against the other mantelpiece some eighteen feet opposite. The secretary, or minute-taker (someone who can write legibly and quickly), sits next to the chairman on the floor and takes the minutes in a foolscap ledger.

I will get to do this job when I'm older. It is a privilege accorded the older kids and taken very seriously.

Chairman: 'OK, everybody, quiet down! Tribunal. Carole, will you read it off?'

Kids are yawning, sighing, sprawling, knitting. Tinies are misbehaving. Those who are clingy attach themselves to an adult, like love-starved apes. We are always cold in the winter, cuddling up to each other under an army blanket. Here in the lounge, sitting on the floor during meetings, older kids hug younger ones, and the little ones cuddle in to them. It's considered anti-social not to attend, and 'anti-social' is the worst thing you can be accused of.

Neill is the only one with a chair. He sits, sucking occasionally on his pipe, which is unlit, so he is continually fiddling with it. He wears a corduroy jacket or suit in clement weather, tweed when it's colder, and when it's very cold, he keeps his overcoat on, and usually his flat cap.

Carole (secretary): 'Van versus Sean for going down the fire escape. One and a half hours of work for Sean in the garden.'

Chairman: 'Right. Are there any appeals? Sean?'

Sean: 'I want to appeal that fire escape bit. I had no idea you weren't allowed on the fire escape.'

Larry: 'Hey, look at him, will you? Wow! Real sharp!'

Chairman: 'OK, quiet down, you two. You didn't know, Sean?'

Sean: 'I didn't know, so do what you want I'm telling you, I didn't know the law.'

Millie: 'Look, he knew, 'cause it happened to Larry a few weeks ago, and Sean was here at the meeting. I think the fine should stick.'

Chairman: 'All right. Now look, if you want to talk, raise your hand, OK? We'll vote on it. All in favour that Sean gets let off.'

Neill: 'For what? I can't hear; you people make so damn much noise.'

Chairman: 'He was fined an hour and a half of work in the garden for going down the fire escape. All right. All in favour he is let off. All against. Sorry, mate, the fine sticks. Any more appeals?'

I look across the room at Sean. My green eyes meet his blue grey ones and I feel a mixture of sadness and shame. Myles has volunteered a mentoring role. He'll look out for Sean, he says. Like Chrissy, Sean has discovered the pottery shed. Sean learns quickly. He's ambidextrous. He centres the clay confidently, all the time keeping the wheel spinning with his footballer's leg. Throws water over the clay to keep it slippery and moist, he makes a hole with his thumb, all the time turning and shaping with both hands.

He's good at this. He uses every bit of his hand – the palm, the knuckles, the heel, his fingers. He is praised for his work and gives me a bowl for Christmas glazed a milky turquoise; the base is a little heavy with SC etched into the yellow clay underneath. It's perfectly shaped.

Uncle Tom arrives.

'Did you bring my baseball mitt?' says Sean.

Tom, empty-handed, shrugs apologetically.

I'm bursting with excitement. It's been almost a whole year since he put us on the train to Summerhill. I think he's been so busy custody battling with Grandma Cuddihy that he hasn't had time to come and see us. Chrissy calls custody 'custardy', like the yellow custard we get with our 'pudding'. 'I wonder how the custardy battle is doing?' he sometimes asks me, but none of us know.

Now Chrissy, Sean and I are fidgeting in the corridor outside Neill's office. Uncle Tom has gone inside for his very own PL, or pow-wow, as he calls it. We can hear murmuring and the occasional burst of laughter from my uncle. (Neill must have told one of his jokes.)

He emerges from Neill's office and we are leaping all over him.

I'm bursting with pride as we walk down the stairs, and around the grounds, showing off our uncle to everyone.

See, I want to shout. *He's here. He does exist. It's not just a story I told you in bed. And he's all ours.*

'Get in the car, kids. Let's go somewhere!'

We haven't been in a car all year. There's a bit of a scuffle about who will go in front. Sean wins because he's the oldest, and visibly subdued. Not that Tom notices.

Before long we find ourselves hurtling down narrow Suffolk country lanes. The rented car brushes the lush summer foliage. The car radio is tuned to Cliff Richards (imitation Elvis) singing, 'We're All Going on a Summer Holiday'.

'Great news, your Aunt Joan is going to have a baby,' Tom suddenly announces.

Chrissy and I are jumping up and down on our seats, ecstatic at the prospect of a new cousin, but Sean is quiet.

'Now, calm down, you two,' Tom says soberly. 'You don't understand. Joan's not having a baby with *me*. We decided that our friend, Saul, would be a more suitable father so we went along to his place in Amagansett, and talked it over with him and his wife, and they agreed.'

The excitement we've been feeling turns to puzzled disappointment, and we remain silent for the rest of the journey.

We drive to Aldeburgh and go and see *Lawrence of Arabia*. Afterwards, walking on the beach, Sean and Chrissy search for flat stones to skim across the foamy grey water. I'm holding my Uncle's hand, looking out to sea.

'When can we go home?' says Sean.

It's the question that's been on our lips all year.

'Look kids,' says Uncle Tom. 'Summerhill *is* your home now.

I want you to think of Ena and Neill as your parents, well, your foster parents, anyway.'

'But can't we come back? Even for a vacation?' I ask.

'Well, that depends. There's still some stuff I have to work out with…' He stops. 'Well, let's just say there's some stuff I have to iron out.'

Sean hurls a stone with all his might, it seems to go on for ever, as high as the seagulls, and disappears; he has always been a good pitcher.

'What I need,' says Uncle Tom, 'is for each of you to write to your grandmother and tell her you're happy and settled here. Will you do that, Lizzie, Chrisser-Kev and Seanie? (Tom has given us all nicknames: Deedee is Doodle-Bug, and Bob is Robbie).

'I guess,' I say, 'but why can't Nanny come to Summerhill?'

He doesn't answer.

The next day he leaves for Scotland to see Bob and Deedee (or Robbie and Doodle-Bug). He will have to sit through *Lawrence of Arabia* again, as it's showing at the Castle Douglas Picture Palace.

I soon forget about Uncle Tom's visit.

A group of tinies (Vicky's collective nickname for the littlest kids) are crowded around Neill, asking him questions.

'Neill, Neill! What did the school used to be before you came here?'

'Oh, this was a gentleman's house, with servants. The dining room was a billiard room, with an enormous billiard table, and everyone dressed up for dinner in evening dress.'

'Neill, Neill, wouldn't it be fun if we all dressed up once a week, and had big, velvet carpets running down the stairs?'

'Yes, that's a very good idea,' says Neill and wanders off to take Biscuit for a walk.

There are lots of trees at Summerhill. It's said that the rich industrialist who built the big, Gothic mansion planted every single type. But the Big Beech tree is the only tree that has its own name. It is special, enormous, legendary and full of history, with initials carved from pupils long gone. The overhang from the tree is so big that it feels as if you're entering another world, away from the bustle of the school. In the spring and summer, a canopy of green leaves shimmers above you and in the autumn, there's a soft red carpet beneath your feet.

Way up high, in the 'v' of two branches sits a wooden plank, and hanging from a branch above, a huge rope with a loop at the end. Someone on the ground flings the rope up to you. You must grab it firmly with both hands, put one foot in the loop and push yourself off with the other, swooping, swinging, gloriously, back and forth.

It's taken me a good part of a summer to get up the courage to jump. I've had several goes at climbing the little wooden struts nailed to the side of the tree, up to the plank, and just sitting there.

'Come on. Get on with it!'

Vicky and Vaar, down below, yell encouragement. Inevitably I have to climb down again, backwards, like a film playing in reverse.

Finally, after umpteen attempts, I manage it. There is no stopping me now. My fear has gone. Until the next year, when I have to work up the courage all over again.

Autumn term, my second year at Summerhill. We decide to play fuck-chase. It is a beautiful crisp day, with a blue sky, and golden leaves on the ground. Vicky gets hold of Hector, Eleanor's little brother. We hold him down, and, as he thrashes among the leaves, Vicky forces him to kiss her. Then he starts crying, so we leave off. He runs away, yelling that he's going to bring us up in the next meeting for bullying. Vicky and I are laughing so hard that tears are running down our faces.

Adam catches hold of Evie (she hasn't run very fast), and he is lying on top of her. He is making some grotesque, comical movements, a horrible parody of grown-ups *doing it*, with all their clothes on. He's grunting like a pig and Evie is squealing like a lady pig. Evie decides there should be a baby, and little Jimmy (one of the tinies) is commandeered. She wraps him in the ragged old baby blanket that he carries around with him as a comforter. She puts him, struggling, into a wheelbarrow for a pram. He is only four years old and very small so he makes quite a convincing baby. Then we light a fire and try to cook some potatoes that we have dug up from the school allotment, but they burn right through, which is disappointing.

There's a wedding in the dining room with Eleanor officiating as the priest. With her cut-glass accent and perfect command of the English language, she is very convincing. Her pink National Health specs lend her a certain gravitas.

'Do you, Adam, take Evie as your lawful wedded wife?'

He does.

They exchange rings; curtains rings from the sewing room cupboard.

Adam and Evie have appointed themselves our parents. They are officially Mr and Mrs Brown and we are their children. They boss us around and make us do chores, real and imaginary. We collect firewood for the fire, sweep the floor of our makeshift house, built that morning from discarded bricks, corrugated iron and fallen branches, and we do some imaginary ironing, and hang imaginary washing on the imaginary clothes line. We are punished if we don't obey.

The punishments consist of things we have only heard of or read about in *Bunty* and *Judy*; things that happen to other children not as fortunate as ourselves, or if we have experienced them, they are a distant memory. Chrissy is made to stand in a corner, and Vicky, Anna and I have our bottoms smacked with a twig, which Adam calls a 'switch', using quite a convincing Southern accent. We are made to line up and march in formation, 'Hup, two three four,' until it's time to go back to the big house for dinner, smelling of wood smoke.

*

Along with Vicky and quite a few others, Chrissy and I decide that the heavily bevelled mirror in the downstairs toilet is *exactly* what we've been looking for. Everyone seems quite keen to get in on the act. Chrissy and I are happy to exploit our notoriety.

Vicky has a dead sibling, a baby sister she wants to contact as well.

Millie has a much-loved dead grandmother whose legacy has paid for her fees at Summerhill.

We want to talk to Mom.

We lay the mirror out flat, with ourselves gathered around in a circle, our fingers touching an upturned glass that slides around the letters and numbers. A *Yes* and *No*, which Vicky and I have cut out carefully from a newspaper, have been stuck down with little dabs of glue from the art room. We hang blankets around a lower bunk, and light a torch for atmosphere more than anything else. We do our best to conjure up my mother.

Chrissy starts whimpering.

'Hey, what's going on in there?' A long arm reaches in and our blanket cover is blown.

We've managed to frighten ourselves horribly. The next day, Neill has got wind of it, and after discussion in a meeting, the ouija board sessions are banned.

'I'm not saying it's a bad thing, per se, but the dead must be left to themselves,' says Neill, who's known to have dabbled in the occult himself when he was a young man.

I go and tell Ulla but she isn't sympathetic. When pushed, Ulla has a short fuse and quite a temper. Then I remind her about the dress she has promised to help me shorten.

'*Naja*, Mikey, you have ruined it. It is far too short now,' she says.

I flee, laughing, having emptied her waste paper basket upside down in the middle of the room before running away.

'Fucking *Scheissmops*,' she shouts after me.

Her wooden Scholl sandals clomp on bare floorboards.

November, 1963: Vicky, Evie and I are playing with our glass animals in the corridor outside our dormitory. I've bought a new one every week, from a little gift shop in town, with my pocket money handed out by Ena after the General Meeting on Saturdays. I collect a mother deer and then her babies (brown with white spots), cats and kittens (dogs include a delicate poodle with frou-frou legs). We press our noses against the shop window and look covetously at the display, deciding which animal we will buy next.

We've made homes for them in shoeboxes with matchbox furniture. A stack of three makes a chest of drawers. We turn the shoeboxes into 'wagon trains', linking them with string and sliding them carefully along the floor, but the animals topple over anyway.

There's been an earlier, short-lived craze for Barbie dolls. Mine, brought from home, has a curly fringe and a blonde ponytail and she wears a black and white stripy bathing suit. Millie, my Brooklyn friend, has a Barbie, too, with black hair. With her curly black hair, black-rimmed glasses and sloppy sweater, Millie herself resembles a chubby beatnik. She's younger than me by two years, but she's clever, quick and very vocal in meetings.

The English girls, Hannah and Evie, are envious of our Barbies, in spite of the pen marks Chrissy has made on Barbie's legs, which are wearing off. Vicky has a Ken with a dinner jacket he wears for dates with Barbie. He's a little the worse for wear and has developed bald patches on his flock-haired crew cut. We get the dolls to act out seduction scenarios, which eventually collapse into comic rape scenes, plastic clattering against plastic.

At bedtime comes the sound of feet stomping up the stairs. Clancy, an older boy, pops his head in our door: 'Your President's dead. Your President's been shot!'

'*What*…?' I sit up.

Clancy rushes out. I hear him down the hallway, opening doors, shouting his news flash.

'Your President's dead. Your President's dead.' His words echo behind him.

We take the news badly, walking the corridors crying and moping in groups on our beds. For me it's another severance with the past – from a time of hopeful optimism and memories of my mother in her 'KENNEDY FOR PRESIDENT' badge, all red white and blue, pinned to the lapel of her coat.

'The big day isn't long now,' Mom calls out as she leaves the house to go canvassing.

My stepfather has a more sober-looking black and white 'I'M FOR NIXON' button stuck to the lapel of his overcoat. There are lots of heated discussions in our house and raised voices. My mother comes from a long line of Democrats. Both her mother and her father, an eminent New England judge, had been passionate fans of FDR. As for my stepfather, well, Kennedy's too much of a Red for his liking, and you can't trust Catholics. Nixon with his used car salesman looks is much more his kind of guy.

On election morning I wake up to the unfamiliar weekday smell of frying bacon. Mom is in the kitchen, bright and early, cooking up a pile of waffles with maple syrup. She's been up all night watching the votes come in on television, and it looks like Kennedy is going to be our new President. My stepfather has gone to work, slamming the door firmly behind him. We hear the angry revving of the car engine, the furious crunching of gravel as he drives away.

Election fever lingers for some time after Kennedy's inauguration, helped by the Kennedy/Johnson stickers that my mother has stuck to the front and back bumpers of the Packard.

Chapter 9

I know something is wrong. It's the first General Meeting of early February, just inching towards my twelfth birthday, and I haven't seen Sean for three days. I spot Chrissy on the other side of the room and cross my legs beneath me as I tuck myself into the space next to him.

'Sean's gone,' he whispers to me.

'What? Did he run away again? Have they found him?'

'No, he went to that school, the one that Bob and Deedee are at; someone came in a car and took him a couple a days ago.'

'Did you say goodbye? Is he coming back?

'I don't know. I don't think so. He did something bad. He locked Millie in the loo and said he was going to do something to her. Neill told him he had to go. He was crying – a lot!'

I'm devastated. Why didn't he say goodbye? When would we see him again? I hate to think of him crying. Now it's just going to be the two of us here at Summerhill with Bob, Sean and Deedee away in some other place called Scotland, wherever that is. We won't be the Cuddihys any more. When there are three or more of you, you can be an entity. Vicky is Vicky, but she's also a Gregory. Adam Bright is one of the Brights, because there are four of them. Now I'll just be Mikey.

I wish I could speak to my sister but there's no phone at Summerhill apart from the one Neill has in his office. Perhaps I could go to the phone box in town, but I don't have a number for their school. And what would I say? I'm puzzled. No one has said anything about Sean being sent away. I want to say something, but I don't. I can't. So many questions in my head. Why wasn't Sean brought up in the meeting? What did he do exactly and why hasn't it been discussed? We should all have had a vote. (*All those in favour.*) I would have voted for him to stay. I would have put both my hands up in the air and made two votes. Some of the little kids do that, but their vote is only ever counted as one.

The chairman can always tell.

I try to listen to the words in the room but I can't take them in.

Myles: 'I just want to say that no one is allowed out of Summerhill before twelve noon, if they are under fifteen. That's not a Summerhill law, but an English law set by the government, so if you want to break laws, break your own laws. It doesn't do any of us any good to be seen downtown before twelve.'

Joyce: 'That goes for Earl.'

Myles: 'Look, I'm telling everyone. You don't have to take it personally. I would just like all of you to stop it.'

Carole: 'Neill, isn't there a law that no one from Summerhill can go to the coffee bar? There are a few who have been going down there.'

Neill: 'I had that place put off limits because there was a knifing there, and I don't want Summerhill people brought into that kind of thing. There are a lot of labourers around because of the power station in Sizewell, and they are getting drunk and breaking into shops, and I don't want anyone here getting into that kind of thing. This was a law I had to make to protect us all. You have Tufford's café to go to – and the fish and chip shop – that should be enough. I don't want the police down here, telling me that one of you has been hurt. Just stay away from that place.'

Scott: 'I propose a two and sixpence fine for anyone caught down there.'

Chairman: 'Any more business? Right. Meeting closed.'

Sean doesn't write.

But Deedee sends a letter. Her handwriting is small and friendly looking, and she always leaves a large margin on the left hand side of the blue Basildon Bond, almost as wide as the text itself. Usually she crams several sheets into a small envelope; apart from a couple of letters from Bob, they are the only letters I receive with the Queen on the stamp. She writes on the back 'Postman, postman, don't be slow, be like Elvis, go man go.' (She doesn't like Elvis particularly, it's just her sense of humour.) There's some news about Sean, who seems to be 'settling in nicely', and is going to lessons (!)

She writes,

Sean says Hi, and says to give Chrissy a punch on the arm from him. Also, can you tell Leslie (the owner of Tufford's) *that he'll pay him back the 5 shillings he borrowed from the till when he comes to visit.* (He never will visit.) *There's been no word from Tom about the custody battle with Grandma; I can't imagine we'll be sent back to school in America, can you? It'd be nice to go and see everyone though, wouldn't it? Have you heard from Nanette? I had a birthday card from Mimmy last week, and a cheque from Grandma for $20!*

Even though Sean doesn't write, there's still the excitement at the prospect of letters from America. These little blue lightweight airmail envelopes are handed through the serving hatch with our breakfast. I miss Sean, but after a while Chrissy and I seem to settle into calmer waters, into being here, without Sean's running away and disruptiveness.

I take delight in the letters from Mimmy. They are filled with tiny writing, a little bit like her knitting, the stitches are small and perfect. Sometimes she includes a photograph, one of herself and Nanette at Christmas, sitting next to a table with a small, fake tree on top of it, decorated with baubles that are too big for it. Nanny has grown tall and her long, wild hair has been cut short, in a kind of pixie style.

My stepfather Larry sends photos; one of himself in a sharp suit and a pencil thin tie, leaning against a rather nice car, a new Chrysler. Another of his new business, The Southampton Reality Centre, the sign painted with an advertiser's flourish. And then another, of his new family. He married again, pretty quickly.

Nanny sends a letter enclosed in the one from Larry.

We went to Coney Island and Daddy bought Mommy a Moomoo.

'Mommy'?

Nanny has a new mother; I can't imagine having another one, a replacement. It's beyond my comprehension.

My link with the Cuddihys is provided by my uncles, Tom's brothers, the Men of Letters, as I come to think of them. First there's Michael, the youngest, then Jack, the Academic, and then the eldest, Lester, who looks after our Grandmother's 'affairs'.

Uncle Jack is the only real man of letters. He's a professor of sociology at Columbia. He's even published a book – a lengthy tome about the 'Jewish struggle with Modernity'. He sends me my very own copy. As an adult, I will get the book down from my top shelf, blow the dust off, look at the photo of him on the inside cover, taken one faraway summer in Watermill (where the family, in the boys' youth, would spend summers, on Long Island), looking tanned and relaxed, and read through the blurb on the fly leaf: '… an audacious and penetrating thesis…' I read softly, under my breath. I fan through the heavy, cream-coloured pages, *Freud, Marx, Levi-Strauss, Hegel,* jumping out from the densely typeset pages at frequent intervals, interspersed with *Jews, Jewish, Judaism, Yiddish, Zionists, Communists,* and then return it, with a sigh, to its resting place for another few years.

Uncle Jack lives with his wife Heidi in a ramshackle, rent-controlled apartment in Greenwich Village, with three children, and an impressive collection of paintings by some of the leading Abstract Expressionists (he shared the same therapist as one of them). It's Jack who keeps the family 'archive' of photos and newspaper clippings that I discover years later on a trip to New York.

In his study hangs a framed photo of my Great-Grandpa Murray the inventor, with his luxuriant mustache and straw boater, standing on the steps of a big building next to Thomas Edison, with Walter Chrysler to his left. They are celebrating something, perhaps the setting up of their new enterprise, The Edison Illuminating Company. (My uncle has written their names carefully in blue fountain pen over each of their heads.)

Another framed photo of my grandmother as a young bride, standing on the grand hallway stairs of her father's house on St Mark's Avenue in Brooklyn. Her bridal train, spilling down the stairs, falls into a pool of satin several feet below her. Much later, this photo will appear on the cover of *Real Lace*, a book about 'America's Irish Rich', written by Stephen Birmingham, in the 1970s, along with several other family photos inside.

And here's another photo of the whole clan in Southampton at my Great Grandfather Murray's house. The year is 1929: Lufkins, McQuails, McDonnells, Cuddihys, Murrays taken as a panorama, revealing a tumbling line up of thirty-six grandchildren: toddlers to adolescents, the girls in starched summer dresses, bows in hair, the boys in shorted suits with their hair slicked down. One or two of the older children inexpertly hold a bundled baby in their arms.

My father is a blur. My uncles say he never stood still.

There are newspaper clippings too, carefully arranged in a scrapbook. I pore over the yellowed pages of the *New York Times*. Here's a photo of my mother and father, cut out from the society pages, looking like startled teenagers:

> Sailing the Social Seas: Robert Cuddihy, cousin to both Mrs Henry Ford and Mrs Alfred Vanderbilt, took a vow three years ago when he married Betsy Ryan that he wouldn't drink anything stronger than ginger ale. However, the other night in Armando's, the Cuddihys mutually agreed that abstinence should be in abeyance where family celebrations are concerned. So, Bob and Betsy, who have just returned from Havana, clinked champagne glasses in hello-and-farewell toasts to Bob's brother, Jack Cuddihy, who sails soon for Oxford, England…

My father's favourite brother was Michael, the youngest. He will go on to write an unpublished memoir, *The Iron Lung*. After he was struck down with polio, the family hadn't expected him to survive, and as my mother and father were expecting their fourth child, me, they decided to name the baby, regardless of gender, after him. My uncle and I have a special bond. He's my godfather and takes his role very seriously.

In his memoir, he recalls waking from the long and painful fever, 'like a swimmer surfacing from a deep pool'. An old priest, with 'a shock of white hair and ruddy face', is standing over the iron lung, performing the last rites, his mother dressed completely in black, with a lace mantilla covering her hair, as if he was already dead. The priest has just anointed him, making the sign of the cross with his thumb, on Michael's forehead, ears, nose and mouth.

'I'm not going to die Father,' protests Michael, with all the strength he can muster.

Michael spends a year in the iron lung and the rest of his life paralyzed from the waist up, in need of constant care. When I was little, visiting my Grandmother Cuddihy in her Park Avenue apartment with my father, I begged for rides on his rocking bed, a motorized contraption that rocks up and down to help his lungs move. Moving to Arizona where the dry climate is more suited to his health, he publishes an influential poetry quarterly, and translates French philosophical texts into English. He even sends me $50, a share of a royalty cheque from his first published collection of poetry, during my early years as a struggling artist in East London. During those years, he writes me encouraging letters.

The envelope, headed with authority, 'Great Britain and Air Mail', holds the promise of a wonderful letter inside, typed densely on both sides, by an assistant, and sometimes 'a little something' enclosed.

June 1987

Dear Mikey,

Your letter, your very good letter, has been with me for several weeks now. I love your handwriting and the wonderful way you help me to picture you in your studio, a proper setting for an artist of your calibre. I love studios; the way the space liberates you from all your smallness. Everything becomes possible in that instant when you feel yourself enlarge.

… I love the way you use adverbs (sporadically, initially, finally); entire lines of handwriting shift in place like waves, breaking on the beach at Watermill.

And then, with his barely useable left hand, he signs the letter:

Love, Mike

The eldest of the brothers, my Uncle Lester, is married to the ex-governess of his younger brothers and sisters, my delightful Tante Gabby. As we get older, and he takes over the reins from my Uncle Tom, his letters become more frequent. He types by the 'hunt and peck' method, as he calls it. I imagine him sitting at his desk, chewing his cigar as he concentrates on the keyboard.

Now where's that darned p?

His letters launch into news about various family members that always include speculative statistics: a nephew's salary; his son's probable alimony payments to his estranged wife; a description of someone's illness with all the gory details. A surprisingly handy tip passed on from Tante Gabby about how to cook mashed potatoes: the best way to make them is to put them through a mouli, add 'scalding' milk, and finally, the butter. Sometimes, Gabby adds a postscript by hand, in her loping French scrawl:

> *'Allo Michelle, je souhaite que vous ayiez un bon été,*
>
> *Bien affectuesment, Tante Gabby*

We are waiting at the front of the school building for Grandma to arrive. In spite of assurances that there will be no kidnapping, our passports are locked away in Neill's office, for safe keeping. According to Deedee, Uncle Tom has reached a truce with my grandmother and the custody battle is winding down. I imagine gun slingers lining up on either side of the courtroom. My grandmother and my aunts and uncles on one side of the room, and my uncle Tom, with Aunt Joan and my uncle's friends (the seven men from the airport, maybe, along with Saul and his hypodermic needle) on the other. Letters are produced as evidence (the pen is mightier than the sword!): my Uncle Jack writes a long letter to the judge, declaring Tom 'erratic and unreliable', but then Uncle Tom produces the letters we've written home.

The result of this is that Grandma has finally been convinced that we are happy and no longer wants us to come and live with her.

We don't expect a Rolls-Royce, complete with liveried chauffeur, to crunch up the drive but here she comes. She has sailed over on the *Queen Elizabeth* with her companion, Miss Elsie. The whole school, all the little kids anyway, crowd around the shiny black vehicle like Third World orphans. I feel proud and embarrassed at the same time.

'You poor children,' says Grandma Cuddihy, and the unfamiliar softness of her mink coat brushes against my cheek, as she hugs me to her, and I take in the unmistakable scent of Chanel No. 5.

Ena sends us to the bathroom to wash our faces, get toothbrushes, and change one pair of patched jeans for another. Chrissy has gone feral. He seems to spend most of his time building dens in the woods and climbing trees. His face is black with dirt and he smells of wood smoke.

We are taken off in the Rolls-Royce to a posh hotel in Aldeburgh, the nearest big town, for a few days' R & R. The food is great. We can order anything we want to eat. The atmosphere is a million miles away from the anarchy of the school dining room, where food is shoved at you through the serving hatch, and platters of mouldy, homemade brown bread sit ready 'marged' and rejected; where two plastic washbasins hold slopped out food which you scrape your leftovers into, to be fed to the chickens.

At the hotel, there are white tablecloths with matching damask napkins so thick they don't crease, and silver cutlery, which gives a muffled, not a clattering sound, on the table's covered surface. Everything is covered: a stifling softness of carpet, cushions, curtains. There is no shouting, only the quiet, murmured conversation of the other guests in the background. We can have anything we want, except fun. The atmosphere is polite, oppressive.

My appalling stammer is made worse by the formality of the place, and the fact that we have to be on our best behaviour and not swear or shout. To get through sentences, I punctuate them with, 'Oh God', at regular intervals. Grandma, who has a very dry sense of humour, suggests I substitute, 'Oh God' for 'St Francis', or someone of a lesser order, but I can't manage anything else. God is the best I can do.

Miss Elsie is reading the *Daily Telegraph*. There is an article, about Enoch Powell who has just been appointed shadow something or other, and he is beginning to be vocal about 'the evils of the colour question in this country'.

'Well, I have to say, this Enoch Powell person seems to have some interesting opinions. I like the sound of him…'

I don't like the Conservatives. None of us at Summerhill like them. If they win the next election, we are convinced they will close our school down and send all black people and foreigners back to wherever they might have come from. I can feel myself going red in the face, but I remain silent, inwardly fuming at Miss Elsie, and frustrated by my lack of words. I suspect my grandmother doesn't like Miss Elsie very much either.

Grandma Cuddihy is a petite woman, not given to excessive emotion. A remote figure, she never hugs her grandchildren, just a sideways air kiss so as not to interfere with the Elizabeth Arden lipstick (a particular shade of coral) and immaculately coiffured peroxided hair. She still lives in righteous splendour in the elegant apartment block on the corner of 89th and Park Avenue commissioned by her father-in-law, R.J. Cuddihy, a publishing magnate. The building boasts an immense courtyard, unusual for Manhattan's Upper East Side, half an acre of precious greenery, startling amongst the height and bustle of stone and metal, with a central fountain. Rays of sun reach down to the leafy idyll.

It's rumoured that the publishing millionaire's Irish origins had excluded him from the higher echelons of Madison Avenue, so he took his money and built his own apartment block in 1925. My grandparents moved into the building in 1946, downsizing from the five-storey brownstone on East 73rd Street, which they'd occupied since their marriage. My Uncle Mike and his sister Anne-Marie were the only children living at home by then, the others had flown the nest.

Some of this I know. The rest I will acquire from Deedee and Bob in the years to come.

There is something unknowable about my grandmother yet something about her makes me think she would be fun under different circumstances.

Chrissy and I are pleased to get back to school with a ten shilling note each in our pockets, back to heating up our breaktime milk over illegal stoves, tree climbing, and whispering to friends in our dormitories. Perhaps this is because we've forgotten what it is to have a real home, a family home. Instead Summerhill feels like home.

By the following summer our greatest wish has become our greatest fear: that Grandma might send someone to steal us and send us to a strict Catholic school back in America.

Chapter 10

The Americans at Summerhill outnumber the English kids, two to one. Most of the kids seem to be from California, lots of suntans and white blonde hair. My favourite 'newcomers' are the Brights – although they arrive just a term after us; on a frozen February afternoon, with their mother: a family of four kids from Santa Barbara. A single bed is added to our dormitory for Anna. The Bright family have an eccentric sense of style that sets them apart from everyone else. Their parents, Marion and Steve, are both actors, and the Bright children all speak with rather affected Anglo-American accents, enunciating each word very carefully. They are avid collectors of junk-shop paraphernalia.

Nathan, the eldest at fifteen, has bad acne and a strange greasy fringe. The older girls tease him mercilessly. He makes papier maché puppets and puts on shows for the school. One of the puppets, a princess, cries real tears (fake jewels that clatter from her eyes onto the floor). He's made his own portable theatre, which folds out into three sides, painted with wide stripes of red and yellow. There are curtains, too, which pull back properly. Sometimes his sister, Anna, helps him operate the puppets. They have incredible costumes.

Stephen, at thirteen, a quiet redhead with a haircut like a Shakespearean prince, is a brilliant classical guitarist. And then there is Anna (who I share a dormitory with) and Adam, her twin. Adam knits elaborate Arran jumpers, fashioning extraordinary cables and knots, which grow at an amazing rate from long, clacking metal needles, which he tucks under his arms. He's always sitting there, knitting, on Ulla's bed, in his cut-off jeans and T-shirt, his long Monkees fringe obscuring his eyes.

Anna speaks in a whisper so you have to lean in close to hear her. She keeps the room awake at night with a nagging cough that never seems to go away. Although no one says so, we think it's psychological, as she seems fine during the daytime. She is the palest of the Bright children with a purplish pallor and long, red gold hair. She looks like a sixteenth-century princess, something out of a Holbein painting.

I see her going into Neill's office for a PL and wonder if she's going to talk about her cough.

She keeps us up again that night.

One day Anna brings back a wind-up gramophone with spare needles in a little hidden drawer, and 78s in brown paper sleeves. I learn to sing all the words to Stanley Holloway's scratchy 'Anne Boleyn': *'With her 'ead tucked underneath 'er arm, she walked the bloody tower…'*

I wonder how the oldest Brights, Stephen and Nathan, who are both well over twelve years of age, have managed to get in here. Perhaps they haven't been damaged. They are a close-knit family with a mother who comes to visit a lot. Again, I'm mystified. Wouldn't it be nicer to live at home, with your parents?

As well as the Bright family, there's Mitch who wears Brooks Brother's shirts and chinos, instead of the regulation tapered jeans like the rest of us. Mitch brings me Jefferson Airplane records when he returns from holidays in California, and Hershey's kisses (little cones of chocolate covered in a twist of silver paper).

In contrast to straight-talking Mitch, there is Suzanne, who arrives a couple of years after me. Also from Los Angeles, she's the daughter of (at least one) psychiatrist. Suzanne is a creature from another planet. She has violet coloured eyes and long black hair and she washes her skin with Japanese washing grains. She lets me try some. Yes, my skin feels softer afterwards. As part of her beauty routine, she eats powdered yeast mixed with tap water, which she also lets me try. It's horrible.

'I had my first tab of LSD when I was ten,' she tells us.

Is this why she tells everyone she loves them?

I don't ask.

Instead I watch as she glides by like a psychedelic dream. Suzanne is one of the beautiful people we read about in the newspaper headlines that Olly pins up on the notice board alerting us to current affairs. We gaze at photos of people with long hair and flowers in their hair, dancing at a pop festival in California. Heading through the sixties, these beautiful people even appear on the cover of *Time Magazine*. We watch Scott McKenzie singing on *Top of the Pops*, '*If you're going to San Francisco, be sure to wear some flowers in your hair…*'

Some of the beautiful people pitch up at the school in VW camper vans with 'Ban the Bomb' signs and flowers painted on the doors. Smiling couples stroll the grounds, arm in arm, as if they are visiting Monet's Garden at Giverny. They've read all about Summerhill and want to see a 'free' school for themselves. But we give them short shrift.

'Oi. What are you staring at?'

They find the school surprisingly drab. We are not the flower children they were expecting to find. We are scruffy little tykes, running around the place, climbing trees, swearing, and wrestling each other to the ground.

Despite this influx of American culture, I feel myself gradually losing my American self. But I fight it. English jeans are made by Jet not Levi's and Cliff Richards seems inauthentic. He's not even ersatz American, he's just pathetic. All of these things make me long for the things we've left behind. They make the lack of American culture worse than ever. My America is borrowed from my school friends. My lived experience is banished to memory, old-fashioned and faded, prompted by the out-of-date movies we see at the local cinema. Sitting in the dark, eating damp Smiths crisps with their damp little twist of salt in blue wax paper; they bear no resemblance to American potato chips.

*

Aunt Joan appears in a film called *Hands of a Stranger* at the Leiston Picture House. The Leiston Picture House is a second run cinema, showing films that have been out for a while. Cinema nights are twice a week, Tuesdays and Fridays. On Tuesdays, we get crisps with our tea, which we save to take with us and eat in the cinema. *Hands of a Stranger* is in black and white; it's a B-movie about a concert pianist who loses his hands in an accident, and has them replaced by the hands of a murderer, and then goes mad. Aunt Joan plays his terrified wife, and suddenly there she is on the screen, larger than life. I show her off to my friends who have come along to see her. This is almost better than Grandma and her Rolls-Royce.

But, of course, it's only a film, not even a soap opera, so she can't signal to us like she used to. And she's not going to come home later that evening. Does she even think about us any more? She seems to have disappeared from our lives completely. There are no letters or presents or phone calls from Joan. If I think about her too much, I feel sad so I train myself *not* to. Simple as that.

'OK, kids. Take one.'

(A man in a stripy jumper shuts the clapperboard.)

Now it's our turn in front of the camera. December 1964, and Anglia TV are making a documentary about Summerhill. As instructed, we play up to the cameras under the delicious warmth of the camera lights. Little kids wrestle on the floor and chase each other around the room. Even the older kids are rough-housing. All the older photogenic kids are crammed into an older kid's room to look the part. Are we pretending to be the next generation of beautiful people, I wonder.

Someone has been persuaded to play 'Where Have all the Flowers Gone' on the guitar with everyone singing along. Everyone starts jiving. We don't stop. We dance for hours in a kind of trance. The rhythm and exercise are exhilarating. I'm dancing my heart out. My skinny legs in their tapered jeans, skimming across the floor, in a pair of converse baseball boots, leading Evie. Wearing a boy's sweater with a shirt collar poking out, my hair cut in a bob, I look just like a boy. A very happy boy.

Chapter 11

Myles's bedroom is at the top of a winding staircase, leading up from the lounge. It's conveniently located next door to the girls' dormitories (the teenage boys, interestingly, sleep in another building) and it's the only bedroom with a lock on it. I often see him standing by his door, looking through the huge bunch of keys he carries with him, searching for the right Yale. Myles is a charmer, popular with adults and children alike. Kneeling down with a load of little kids, he takes his turn at jacks, which we play on the splintery wooden floors. He is short and beer-bellied, dark haired, with Ena's gypsy colouring. He wears handmade collarless shirts in tasteful muted stripes, and American jeans.

A huge double bed takes up most of the space, raised off the floor, with cushions and a Scandinavian duvet. Posters for jazz festivals decorate the walls. There's an enormous hi-fi with a tasteful collection of records, everything from The Swingle Singers murmuring Bach hysterically, to the latest from the Beatles or the Rolling Stones. A clique of kids hangs out in his room and smokes. He provides the cigarettes, flinging them to his favourites among us.

'Here. Catch.'

I'm not part of the clique that hangs out in there on his bed. I'm not even a smoker. But I love listening to the music that escapes from underneath his door.

Every Thursday at 7.30 p.m. Myles sets up his portable black and white television in the library. We all crowd in. Little kids sit cross-legged on the floor in front. Those of us standing spill out of the doorway into the corridor. We watch *Top of the Pops* and then *The Man from Uncle*. No one is allowed to speak. If they do, the whole room goes 'SHUUSH,' in one loud, whispered voice.

A year before Sonny and Cher appear on the television singing 'I Got You Babe' (followed closely by Ike and Tina's 'River Deep Mountain High'), I invite derision from my friends when I go downtown to the shops and spend my seven shillings and sixpence on a single by Gigliola Cinquetti. I fall in love with this tiny girl of a woman, with her heavy dark hair in a half ponytail, and a modest flick of eyeliner along her upper lids. Standing all by herself on that huge stage, backed by a massive string section of Mafioso-looking gentlemen, all wearing dark glasses, she oozes cool. As soon as I get my pocket money, the small black disc with its bright blue Decca label in the middle is mine. I learn all the words to both the songs. *'No ho l'età'* ('I'm Not Old Enough') has won the Eurovision Song Contest that year (1964) with a simple, sad sounding ballad. I don't understand the words but I get the feeling. The 'B' side, *'Se un Bravo*

Ragazzo' ('You are a Good Boy') is more upbeat and cheerful – and just as good.

I would love someone to love, but there is no one in the immediate vicinity. We are like siblings, too familiar with one another to contemplate romance.

Suzanne has been seen holding hands with Jake, also from California. Theirs is a serious affair. After bedtime and lights out, Jake is allowed to sleep in Suzanne's bed. Everyone must be in bed by lights out, but there is an unwritten exception to the rule, that girlfriends and boyfriends can sleep together, but it has to be serious. (I'm not sure who decides.) Zoë and Bill (our French teacher) are serious too. They walk about with their arms around each other's waists. Zoë with her gamine haircut has a calm, mature presence and could easily be mistaken for twenty-six instead of sixteen. Bill is sleeping with the boss's daughter yet Neill seems to turn a blind eye, although I will learn later that Neill suffers some anxiety over Bill being a 'lapsed Catholic'. Holly and Pete mostly fight, play punching and chasing each other. Holly has a gentle English glamour. Unusually, she's here on a local authority grant, so her English accent isn't the upper class one I've been used to hearing from Hannah and Eleanor.

I long to be kissed.

I cast my mind back to Long Island, where we lived with Uncle Tom for that short period after Mom died. I am on my way home from school when I see him, the man in the homburg hat. It's

Uncle Fred with his sad droopy eyes, and long grey raincoat, the old-fashioned kind, with big lapels. Uncle Fred is one of a sequence of men, you would call them down and outs, who lived with us, invited by my mother, an enthusiastic member of AA (Alcoholics Anonymous), which was still in its infancy. These men lived singly in the attic, or at the top of whatever rambling run-down house our stepfather had moved us into.

I'm not sure what Uncle Fred ever did. But he starts walking towards me. He stops.

'So sorry to hear about your mother, kid,' he says and holding me by the shoulders, he kisses me on the lips, pushing his lizard tongue inside my mouth.

He smells of whisky. I pull away and run into the house. From the safety of the darkened living room, I see him illuminated by a street lamp, just like in a Hopper painting.

I don't tell anyone.

Instead, at Summerhill, I develop a crush on the Beatles. We all have our favourite. Vicky and Evie love Paul, Hannah and Eleanor love John and I love George (he looks shy). The older girls hold coffee bar nights in their dormitory. The room is transformed with a red light bulb and a record player plugged into one of the light fittings, playing *'Love love me do. You know I love you…'* Lit by the rosy glow of the red light, clutching our camp coffee flavoured with carnation milk, we are transported to another world of romance.

Eleanor (who is fond of cliques), joins the Beatles' fan club, and receives a nifty little badge, which says 'Member – Beatles

Fan Club', a newsletter, and a special poster to put up on her wall. We are all a little envious of the special edition flexi disc the club sends her for Christmas, with John, Paul, George and Ringo joking around, singing Christmas carols and barking like dogs. But we think the candlewick bedspread with the Fab Four embroidered on it, and *Yeah yeah yeah* across the top is taking it a bit far.

After lights out, I lie in bed and listen to the clicketty-clack of Neill's typewriter. Neill's office is on the other side of our dormitory. In the morning as I walk past his room, I catch sight of his typewriter, a surprisingly modern-looking object, rather sleek. Perhaps it was a present from one of his many admirers. The typeface he uses is a friendly one, not your usual 'courier' but 'cursive', so it looks almost like handwriting. I know this because Neill always has a letter on the go. He's like my uncles, a man of letters. Every morning, he carries his stack of post down the path from the cottage, where he lives, to his office in the main building, next to our dormitory, to be read and answered.

Chapter 12

The piano in the staff room is in pretty good nick. Sometimes I'm
allowed to go in there and play it, running over the pattern of tunes
I'd been learning up until Mom's death. The sheet music on top of
the piano is jumbled up. I'm not good at sight-reading, but I work
out a few simple things, a half-hearted attempt at the *Moonlight
Sonata*, but I never get beyond the first few bars and the hidden
desire for someone to teach me.

By the time I realize I can no longer recall the sound of my
mother's voice, it's too late. It's gone. It was the thing that most
defined her. Its absence leaves a void in my head. Mimmy's is the
voice I now recall, high-pitched and quavery, an old lady's voice.
How strange. She sits in an armchair in her room, with her eyes
sparkling, humming along to a tune in her head while she's knitting,
or singing '*Que Sera Sera*' along to the radiogram.

'Night, night, darling.'

Mom is in a hurry, going out somewhere. Before she goes, she
sits on the edge of my bed, running her fingers through my hair

(I don't want her to stop), singing a lullaby, ever so softly.

She dangles a cold necklace, her earrings lightly brushing my cheek as she leans over to kiss me goodnight, rustling off to give a recital somewhere.

I've been forced to share a room with Jemima for a term. The room is tiny, partitioned with plywood to make an even tinier room. These rooms are considered a promotion for older girls, from communal dormitories to something more private.

Petite and glamorous, Jemima arrives three years after me, wears her brown hair cut into a sleek helmet at Vidal Sassoon's. She's fourteen, a year older than me, but she might as well be eighteen. Aged thirteen, I have my own hair singed, once a term, with a wax taper at the local barber's for sixpence, and have yet to see the inside of a real hairdresser's. Jemima wears a short 'vest dress' from Biba with wide, alternating stripes of purple and black. She sports dark glasses and flirts outrageously with the boys, and the male teachers for that matter.

At night, in my narrow metal bed, I try not to listen to Jemima giggling with her boyfriend after lights out. Even buried under my blankets I can still hear them kissing and fumbling.

I roll over.

Jemima, across the darkness, sneers:

'Poor Mikey, snivelling under the covers, with no boyfriend. How *pathetic* you are.'

Later that summer, I'm asked to take Jemima's little brother,

David, to London for a haircut. I'm not sure why Jemima hasn't been asked. Her mother, Laura, meets us at Liverpool Street Station. I stay the night with the family in a beautiful house in Hampstead, and the next day Laura takes me to Biba, which is like taking me to Mecca. She buys me a dress with bell-bottom sleeves, in soft cream cotton, patterned with tiny black flowers. It's only a few inches above my knees, but feels daringly short, and of course, I wear it out of the shop immediately. Wolf whistles and beeping car horns follow my progress down Kensington Church Street. I'm embarrassed and thrilled at the same time.

The autumn brings little Rebecca De Mornay from Santa Rosa. Even at five years old, she's a Hollywood star and insists on referring to herself in the third person, as if she's in a film:

'Oh no, not rice pudding again, said Rebecca angrily.'

Pretty soon she blends in with the tinies, all permanently shod in wellingtons with trousers tucked in, and ragged jumpers, snotty and frayed at the cuffs, and anoraks which they wear indoors as well as out. In the summer, they strip down to dirty grey vests, still with their trousers and their wellingtons, caked with dried mud. But Rebecca doesn't entirely loose her sparkle. Her blonde hair, tied back in an untidy braid, seems to radiate light. She's often in the art room, playing with clay, chatting away to herself, or cutting pictures out from magazines and sticking them onto a piece of paper.

Rebecca has taken a shine to Vicky and follows her around like a puppy. Vicky, with her maternal instincts, takes pity on the tinies, poor freezing little things, and makes cocoa for them on a methylated spirit stove. They crouch around hopefully while it's heating.

My new best friend is Valerie Moss from California. With her white blonde hair and pert features, we are opposites; like night and day. She is quick and clever and deft at the guitar. She has two LPs by Joan Baez that we listen to over and over again. Most of the songs seem to involve murder, suicide, unrequited love, and often end with digging someone's grave both wide and deep. Val and I haven't been in love or jilted, yet we identify with the songs' themes of loss and abandonment.

Ena has bought me a guitar for my thirteenth birthday and I set about, with Val's instruction, learning some of the songs on her albums. 'Donna Donna', about a calf being taken to market and slaughtered, is the first one I master, in A minor and E, with a G thrown in for the chorus. Vicky returns from Portland with a guitar too and teaches us a mawkish song, 'Dead Little Girl of Hiroshima': '*I come and stand at every door, but none can hear my silent tread; I knock and yet remain unseen, for I am dead, for I am dead…*'

The guitar becomes my solace, my constant companion.

We sit in one another's rooms, legs dangling from the top of a bunk, our fingers carefully, inexpertly, on the fretboard, strumming clumsily. Pretty soon I develop calluses on the fingertips of my left hand and can form some of the chords without looking.

*

'You're kidding me. That's not *her*...

I'm sitting on the stairs with Val, watching through the banisters. Rumour has it she's run away from Bob Dylan after a bitter row on tour with him, and here she is, pitched up at our school, looking just like she does on her record covers. Beautiful, dainty, dark-skinned and elegant, in her jeans and velvet jacket, her long hair tied back low on her neck, silver earrings dangling. Totally cool. Totally exotic.

Joan Baez sets up a stool in the lounge and starts to tune her guitar. She puts her guitar down, and climbs up to the gram box and puts a record on. It's 'Baby Love' by the Supremes. The song blares out of the speakers at opposite corners as Joan starts singing in a pop-star soprano, just like Diana Ross, only better somehow. The French windows seem to vibrate with the sound of her voice. We have all her records and here she is, dancing and twirling exuberantly in her bare feet as if she is one of the Supremes on *Top of the Pops*.

We decide to nip upstairs and get our instruments.

Val is pushier and more outspoken than me. I trail along behind her, my heart pounding.

'Hey,' says Joan, a smile lighting up her face as we approach with our guitars.

Val says, 'Hi. Could you teach my friend and me some guitar picking? We've worked out the chords for 'House Carpenter', but we want to know how you do the finger-picking bit.'

'Well,' she says, rolling her eyes in mock exasperation, 'I'm not sure if I should be giving trade secrets away to the competition.'

'What's your name, honey?' she addresses me. I tell her. 'Unusual name for a girl. Are you from the US, sweetie? Where from? My, you're both a long way from home.'

'Well, let's see. Are we all in tune?'

Val is, but my guitar is at least a semitone out. Joan takes it from me and gets it sorted, leaning her head to one side to hear, her forehead furrowed with concentration as she adjusts and turns the pegs with her delicate caramel fingers.

And then she shows us. First she gets us to beat a rhythm back and forth with our thumbs, alternating the three bass strings, and once we've got that right, picking up the top 'high' strings in between, like weaving, until, very soon, we are playing, keeping up the rhythm with her while she sings along.

> *'Well met, well met, my own true love,*
> *Well met, well met,' cried he.*
> *'I've just returned from the salt salt sea,*
> *All for the love of thee'*

Joan stays for a few days, hanging out at the school in the daytime, and spending the night at a local B&B. She shows me a sort of Spanish style strum, which is useful for more melodramatic pieces, like '*Té Amor*'.

Later on she gives a concert for all of us in the grubby dining room. Tables have been pushed to the side, but the remnants of peas and mashed potato are still stuck to the floor from lunch, and the not very good Picasso-esque murals painted on the walls by

Harry Herring, the art teacher. Joan plays all our favourites, 'House Carpenter', 'Mary Hamilton', 'Wildwood Flower', as well as one she's picked up in a pub along the way: *'Look at the tombstone, bloody big boulder...'*

Joan likes the school so much she sends her nephew and her godson, Kurt, both to Summerhill. With the proceeds from a London concert, she even pays a substantial contribution towards a new outdoor swimming pool.

Myles spends the best part of the following year supervising and building the pool. We see him either pushing a wheelbarrow, or standing by a noisy cement mixer, shovelling cement.

The water is a deep California turquoise, quite different from the brown grey sea we swim in at Sizewell. It's almost as cold as the sea, but the turquoise makes the water look warmer.

Everyone swims naked.

Ulla goes for an early morning swim, leaving her Scholls at the side of the pool, and does some quiet lengths. I hate seeing the grown-ups so exposed. There is something ugly, wasted and obscene about Neill's red genitalia, flapping about, and Ulla's empty breasts, her sparse, grey pubic hair and wrinkled stomach (I look away, embarrassed). I am horribly self-conscious about my own body and can just about be persuaded to swim topless; to wear a swimsuit would make me more conspicuous, anyway. However, by the end of the summer, I am diving in and out of the pool, with the rest of them, still with my knickers on, but brown and extrovert.

Every summer, as soon as the sun looks promising and there is no imminent sign of rain, we sunbathe in the hockey field (never used for hockey the whole time I am there). We hang out all day on blankets. When it gets very warm, we have classes out there with Bill discussing *Lord of the Flies*. It occurs to me that the boys in the book, stranded on the island, are not unlike the Summerhill boys of between eight and twelve, *gangsters* as Neill calls them, including Chrissy, who seem to be constantly building forts in the woods, and running around with homemade spears and bows and arrows.

I am sunbathing in the hockey field on my own in just my knickers. It's sweltering. Evie and Vicky have gone to the shops to get some Corona, which is cheaper than Coca-Cola or Pepsi. Evie's transistor radio is tuned to Radio Caroline. 'House of the Rising Sun' by The Animals is playing as loud as it can through the static and the waves. I feel a shadow cast itself across my body. I open my eyes. Myles is looming over me, his Pentax clutched between his hands. Adjusting the lens, he points the camera at me and starts shooting, winding the film at top speed between takes, like a photographer at a fashion shoot. I sit up, embarrassed, uncomfortable, my budding awkward breasts, with my hair not quite long enough to hide them.

He wants me to pose.

'Don't be shy. You're a lovely girl. Look this way, come on, do it for Myles. Don't hide. Smile for the camera!'

'No,' I protest. 'I mean I can't.'

I don't feel the least bit lovely. I want to be left alone.

I hope Myles isn't going to pick me as his girlfriend. He always has a girlfriend, changing her every once in a while, picking her out from a giggling group of girls. He auditions them first, checking his jokes out on them, getting them to clean his room for him – I make a particularly bad job of this – or bring him a cup of tea in the morning.

Suddenly, Evie, Vicky and the others appear through a gap in the trees.

'Did you get the Corona?'

Phew. I'm saved.

When Eleanor leaves three years later, after taking her O levels, Myles chooses Sally for his new girlfriend. Sally, big sister to at least three tinies, looks like a child herself with straight hair and dark, oriental eyes. Cut off from her friends, she is marooned with Myles in his room, her own bed in a shared bedroom with Evie just a token space, inhabited by her enormous collection of stuffed animals, which are never disturbed. They seem to wait there for her, on the bed, night after night, jilted, accusatory.

When Sally returns to school after a blissful summer holiday away from Myles, she's promptly greeted by Ena who comes up to her:

'Thank heaven's you're back. Myles needs sorting out.'

My heart sinks.

Chapter 13

Everyone's hooked on *The Lord of the Rings*. A hardback volume in a pale grey cover with a patterned circle on the front lives underneath Anna's arm. I often see her leaning over the book on her bed, her golden hair dangling over the pages. The Brights read out passages to each other.

Nathan, because he is tall and thin and wears dark clothes, is one of the Nazgul, or Dark Riders. He does a good Gollum imitation: *What has it got in its pocketses?*

Nathan and Eleanor greet each other in Elvish: *Bah Elbareth varee a lay!* (May Elbareth protect you).

I remain unconvinced. It's not a world that appeals to me. It's too fantastical. I want something that has a foothold in reality although I like listening to *The Hobbit* being read to us in the evenings by one of the staff.

Oliver Bear has taken to beginning his history lessons by providing everyone around the table with fizzy orange squash, diluted with his state of the art soda siphon (he adds gin to his own glass of orange). Then he reads out the evening's television programmes from the *Radio Times* (he has a television), offering up a whole new televisual world, which consists of *Ready Steady Go*, *The Avengers*, *The Saint* and *Steptoe and Son*.

He offers to teach a group of us how to write in italic script. I love the turquoise ink and the slanted nib of the pen. We lose our curly, American handwriting as we practise the shapes and groups of letters over and over again. I practise writing my name: Michael Elizabeth Cuddihy, making the E in Elizabeth as decorative as I can. Anna copies out an Elvish poem with her pen. It looks pretty good.

Then Oliver gets the wrong idea. Freedom is a funny sort of trap, particularly for young men, I realize before too long. Oliver gets drunk, insanely so, and gropes the older girls. Myles can get away with it; he has a special dispensation; he's Ena's son, part of the inner circle. Oliver's behaviour, however, is considered unacceptable and Neill decides to let him go.

The thing is, I had never expected Oliver to stay. Neill, Ena, Ulla, Olly, Myles and Harry are permanent fixtures; they're part of the fabric of the school, but Oliver, and the others who arrive, fresh and optimistic, are like bit players, making a guest appearance on a long-running soap opera. We all know that their time with us is limited, whether they leave voluntarily to fresher fields, or they are 'let go' (sacked) by Neill is the only thing that's not certain, although I could've taken bets on Oliver being 'let go' within days of his arrival.

*

Aunt Anne Marie is wearing a black shift dress, her blonde hair tied back in a Tom Jones bow. My father's youngest sister, she makes a surprise visit with her husband, David Eaton. Visits from relatives abroad are like visiting hours in an open prison. I long to see my family yet I secretly dread the prospect of confronting a world I've left so far behind. There's no visitors' room to take them to, just a dormitory full of other kids, or the lounge with no chairs and the floor to sit on. Tufford's becomes a kind of reception centre.

Anne Marie is four month's pregnant and smoking with a cigarette holder. She doesn't like me; she finds me priggish. I've been trying to explain how the meetings work.

'You bring people up who've broken a rule, like smoking under age…'

'But that's being a snitch,' she says, stubbing out her cigarette in her slice of Victoria sponge.

She likes my little brother and gives him a cigarette, even though he's only eleven. Before they leave, she wants to buy us something. There isn't much in Tufford's.

'Can I have a Wagon Wheel?'

I don't like Wagon Wheels very much, but at least it's something. We get ten shillings each, a crisp red and white note, to put into our back pockets. And then, 'Bye,' and I never see them again.

When Tante Gabby and Uncle Les come to visit, I wear my dress from Biba. A fat man with a bristle moustache and a bow tie (I never see him without it), Uncle Les always has a good Havana cigar on the go, and there are little burn holes down the front of his short-sleeved polyester shirt where the ash has landed. Gabby is utterly and elegantly French; there isn't an ounce of American in her. She looks like the Matisse painting of his wife in a little straw hat.

Chrissy is wearing his best clothes, including the red corduroy trousers I've made him. I've even done a proper zip with a fly. Chrissy wears them with braces, his hair recently cut into a black pudding bowl. He has become quite beautiful, a pretty boy with his shiny hair and rosebud lips. We sit outside the French doors on the cracked York stone slabs. Uncle Les takes a photo of the two of us. We look very serious. My dress is barely two inches above my knees; it's the shortest thing I've ever worn. I've tied my hair tied back, low on my neck, like Joan Baez. Chrissy has one knee up, leaning his chin on his hand. It seems inappropriate for Les and Gabby to sit on my single bed so we go to Tufford's for tea and toast.

No other family members come to see us.

Where are Larry, my little sister, Nanny, Aunt Joan, Mimmy?

I wonder if we will ever get home to see them – although I am increasingly unsure where exactly *home* would be.

Bob arrives. He's hitch-hiked all the way from Scotland. I'm proud of my big brother, his talk and swagger; he can talk circles round the older boys at Summerhill. He spends time locked with Neill in his office, having his very own PL before being allowed to take me back to Scotland for a jaunt. At thirteen, Neill says I'm old enough, so we hitch-hike all the way. The flat Suffolk landscape I'm accustomed to turns into soft green hills, outlined eventually by low stone walls. The green is spotted with little beige shapes; sheep, some of them with black faces.

Kilquhanity is deep in the countryside, not at the edge of a town, like Summerhill. It's bordered by big yew trees, rhododendron bushes and pine trees. The earth, carpeted with bark and pine needles, gives off a rich, pungent smell. John Aitkenhead, the headmaster, is a much younger and sprightlier version of Neill and he wears a skirt. Well, a kilt with knee socks. Bob idolizes John. He sees John as a better man, and a true Scot. Killy is more authentic, he thinks, less spoilt than Summerhill. There are fewer pampered Americans there; in fact there are hardly any Americans. The kids have to do chores, muck in to keep the little school afloat, unlike the Summerhill kids, who have maids (cleaners) to mop the floors for them.

I hardly recognize Seanie. He's playing football, a match against a local team from Castle Douglas. He shines, scores two goals, with several headers thrown in for good measure. His hair has grown out to his shoulders. He must be six foot tall. I feel like I hardly know him. But it's obvious that Sean has found a home here. The nearest town is five miles away, so it's not easy to drop out and go and play pinball. The English teacher, who is also a keen footballer, encourages him to read plays, and Sean gets to perform. He starts to write poetry. He shows me a little book he's been writing them in.

Nobody wants to live on their own, sleep on their own but me.

Nobody wants to roam on their own, be on their own but me.

Nobody wants to cry on their own, die on their own but me…

The poem is rather sad, but Sean seems happy enough. To be British is cool. A couple of years later, when Sean goes to visit my Uncle Tom in New York, he will phone to say, 'Guess what? I was chased through Kennedy airport by a group of girls who wanted my autograph. They thought I was one of the Stones, or maybe one of The Pretty Things.'

It's nice to feel that Sean has taken on a British persona. Being thought of as British is an asset. It gives him kudos.

Deedee has narrowly escaped being adopted a second time. She's been taken under the wing of the former art teacher, Kim, and his wife Vivienne. When Kim left Kilquhanity to take up a post at another school, with John's permission, they took Deedee out of school and enrolled her at the local comp in Castle Douglas.

News reaches Uncle Tom who fires off a telegram. (Reassuring to know that he can be firm and decisive when required.)

Edith Therese Cuddihy is to be returned to Kilquhanity School immediately STOP I do not give permission for adoption STOP

My sister is secretly relieved. She's fed up with being adopted, and at seventeen, she feels too old for it anyway. Instead she spends every holiday with Kim and Vivienne, and treats their house, just a few miles from the school, like a second home.

'I'm going to be an artist,' she tells me, as we lie side by side in her single bed, remembering the drive-in movie theatre in Long Island where we used to go with Mom.

'After we got the car hitched up to our drive-in speaker, there was usually half an hour before it got dark enough for the movie to begin. That's when we hit the playground.'

I smile with recognition.

'The only problem with leaving the car was finding it again when the movie started and all the lights had gone out.'

I remember (my sister is impressed) that we would unzip the back window of the Packard, which was made of acetate, and sit on the back ledge with our legs dangling inside, looking out over the roof at the big screen, our giant hot dogs and Cokes in front of us.

'Then came the interval. The spotlights would go on. All the couples kissing in their cars would separate. When we were older,' says my sister, 'the bad part was arriving home and being told we were too big to be carried into the house and so we had to get ourselves up to bed.'

When the time comes to say goodbye to Deedee, Sean and Bob, it feels like our family is split into two, physically and emotionally. Them here in Scotland, Chrissy and myself in England, and then of course there's Nanette, with her new mother back in America. I have a pang of sadness that we will never be whole again.

Back at Summerhill, the school has descended into anarchy. It doesn't get dark now until well after nine o'clock. Everyone has stopped obeying the bedtime rules. Older kids wander downtown in the middle of the night; some of them even go as far as the sea, five miles away on bikes commandeered from the younger ones, to swim in the moonlight, although they know it's forbidden.

There has been a spate of thefts. Someone has broken into Evie's tuck box and taken her birthday sweeties, and the ten shillings from her grandmother. Some other kids have broken into the pantry, pulling up floorboards from the dormitory above and hacking through the ceiling. The windows in the woodwork shed have all been smashed in. No one is going to lessons. Everyone sleeps in because they've been awake all night, either running around the building and the grounds, or been kept awake by other kids playing up.

Chapter 14

I'm upstairs in Ulla's room, at the back of the house, sewing, when the floorboards start to vibrate. Footsteps, marching in time, are accompanied by kids singing. The tune is Elgar's 'Pomp and Circumstance', but I recognize it as the theme tune to *Queen for a Day*, a popular quiz show back home on daytime TV. Pete Love, Jim Darling, Stephen Bright, and a few of the older boys, with Eleanor as a camp follower (I never like her much after this), have decided to start a dictatorship. Elgar's tune is their anthem and they've written words to their song.

> *We all love our freedom, freedom doesn't work.*
> *So we're your dictators for the good of you all.*
> *We all hope you like us, for we're good and strong,*
> *We are your dictators, for the good of you all.*

I hear them marching in a noisy line along the corridor, down the backstairs, past the kitchen and the serving hatch. They go out the back door, down to the carriages, back up the path again, and around the back of the building to the front, where they stop. Pete is carrying a clipboard. He has an announcement to make. I am watching now from the big window overlooking the drive, at the top of the stairs. A ragamuffin army of kids are looking up at him.

'It has become apparent to us over the past few weeks that freedom doesn't work. So, we have decided for everyone's well being to take over the running of Summerhill. For your own good, and the good of the school, we are establishing a dictatorship. I am your leader, and Jim Darling is my second in command. Eleanor Meek is my deputy.'

Interesting to have a Love, a Darling and a Meek as dictators, all of them bespectacled, I think to myself.

'From here on in, everyone will answer to me. I will preside over the General Meeting, and there will be no vote. I will make all the decisions for you. We have rewritten the rules, which we have put up on the notice board. Everyone must obey, or they will be punished accordingly. Everyone will rise at 7.00 a.m. sharp for drill at 7.30, outside. Anyone who stays in bed will be fined one week's pocket money. After breakfast, there will be an assembly at 8.30 a.m. in the lounge, where people will be given their orders for the day. From now on, lessons will be compulsory. Anyone found in their room, or in the school grounds during class time will be punished. You must all address me as Sir. Is that clear?'

'Yes Sir!'

It was Pete's idea. He is one of the older boys, an earlier arrival from the States, almost a man. A lanky gentle giant, his black spectacles and deep voice give him a grown-up authority. The little kids use him as a climbing frame and the older girls flirt with him, trading insults and fake fighting. He is very smart, a talented artist and musician; an all-rounder. With everyone disobeying the rules, staying up well after their appointed bedtimes, keeping people awake, and going downtown when they aren't supposed to, Pete has decided to teach everyone a lesson.

Ulla and I retreat back to her room and resume our sewing, in silence.

Two days later and an argument erupts downstairs in the lounge. We can hear shouting. We peer over the banisters, leaning our heads precariously from above, Val, Vicky, Hannah and myself. We can't see much, a glimpse of a baseball boot (Converse). We are too cautious to move to the stairs for a full view, but we can hear the older girls' voices, and can picture them. I admire them, with their long, sleek hair, their womanly bodies, and their self-confidence.

Vicky's bossy big sister is yelling at Pete.

'I'm not taking orders from you or anyone. I don't know why the hell Neill hasn't stepped in and put a stop to this by now. You just assume, with your intellectual superiority, you have the moral high ground, well, you couldn't be more wrong, buster. You and your tinpot dictatorship can go fuck itself.'

Pete's voice is an insistent murmur, so we can't hear what he's saying.

Holly, with her softer English invective, joins in.

'Yeah, that goes for me too. This dictatorship thing is completely

fucked up. You've gone too far. It's just not funny any more, Pete.'
We can hear scuffling, crying, a door slamming. An emergency
meeting is held in the hockey field. News of the meeting is whispered around the school. Meeting in the hockey field at two o'clock.
Don't tell the dictators!

'All in favour that the dictatorship is abolished?'

All hands are raised.

'Right. Carried. We need to call a Special Meeting in the lounge
tonight after dinner, and confront them.'

When the dictators are confronted by everyone, including Neill,
Ena and all the staff, they concede defeat. The dictatorship is over-
ruled and overthrown. When he is presented with our feelings,
Pete is visibly ashamed. You can see it. Everyone wants to speak.
There is a lot of anger. Yes, many of us had abused our freedom,
but when it was threatened, taken away, we fought to get it back.
Pete's so-called lesson is a hard one for all of us, but he has come
off worse than anyone.

A funny kind of peace descends. A few weeks later, a group
of little kids are made to line up in the lounge after the Saturday
meeting.

'What are you doing?'

The tinies shake their heads and shrug.

As with all coups, there's already another more ambitious and
much scarier power-crazed despot waiting in the wings. In this case
it's Matthew Ackerman, another older American boy, with a creepy
fascination for Nazi memorabilia. His companion, Klauss, again

American, is slightly younger than him. Both wear black, with their jeans tucked into their boots: Matthew has some authentic-looking black leather ones with buckles, Klauss wears wellingtons. Matthew is actually Jewish but he has memorized some of Hitler's speeches from *Mein Kampf*.

'*Sieg Heil.*'

They begin practising their salutes, goose-stepping in formation, and singing the German national anthem. Cassy is one of the little kids. She gets swept up in the role-play; she's not sure what's going on exactly but it seems like a fun kind of game at first.

Ulla takes to her room. We hear the tinies begging, pleading to be left alone. They're fed up with being bossed around and want to leave.

They aren't allowed to. Cassy and her friends are locked in the coal cellar by Klauss. At this point it becomes clear to the whole community that this is not an exploration into freedom – or teenage theatrics.

'This is a fascist coup by a couple of bullies,' says Kat when a second Special Meeting is called.

'But he's not serious,' say some of the older kids, trying to defend Matthew. 'I mean, he's so out there, he's kind of funny.'

But the little kids have been terrorized. Ulla and Harry are visibly upset. The war is a very recent memory. Ulla and Harry are exiles; they have lost their families and loved ones because of Hitler. Some of Neill's colleagues and former pupils in Germany lost their lives in the camps.

Both Matthew and Klauss are condemned by the whole community, which is punishment enough in itself. The episode is considered too serious for a mere fine, and Neill is left to deal with them privately.

Matthew is expelled. Or so we're led to believe.

A few years later, living in Edinburgh, the phone rings. I hesitate, reluctant to pick up. Phone calls are traumatic. There's often a long stammering silence before I can introduce myself. Sometimes this leads to the recipient hanging up before I can get the words out.

It's Evie.

'Have you heard?'

'No. What?'

'Neill received a parcel bomb in the post. It was traced back to Matthew Ackerman. Remember, the Nazi nut? Apparently he's been living as a recluse in a tiny room in San Francisco. The walls were papered with photos and articles, about Neill.'

I find it difficult to believe that Neill, a kind-hearted pragmatist, could inspire this kind of violence.

'I never liked Matthew,' says Evie.

'Me neither. What a weirdo.'

'Anyway, how's things?'

Chapter 15

At the end of term, parents and ex-pupils come to visit the school. They crowd into Ulla's room, bringing presents of wine, whisky, chocolates. Her visitors are given exclusive seats by the gas fire, and I envy them their conversation. Ulla's room is suddenly out of bounds, all sewing put away. Suddenly we are children, second-class citizens, and not welcome.

Myrtle, Evie's mum, is Summerhill royalty. A child here herself, she considers the school her second home. At the end-of-term parties, she sweeps in with her musicians, a carload of scruffy men with an assortment of musical instruments. They are gritty and glamorous with wild hair, leather jackets and pierced ears. They are a perfect foil for Myrtle, who has a vibrant sexy presence. Her dark hair is tied back in the longest pigtail I've ever seen, right down to her bottom. She's not conventionally pretty, but she's striking. She wears long skirts, with coloured petticoats sticking out from the bottom, and laced up leather 'witches' boots. When it's cold, she has a policeman's cape tied over her shoulders, fastened with a silver chain. Sometimes she wears her hair long, with a scarf tied around it, gypsy fashion.

They all smoke black, hand-rolled cigarettes.

I like Hickory Mick the best. He plays the clarinet, which has a beautiful, mellow sound. They liven up Olly's little jazz band made up of my little brother on tea-chest bass, giving it his all, Pete on piano, Nicky Barnet on guitar, Olly with her trombone. Someone has a washboard with thimbles on their fingers. If I'm lucky, I'm given the job of playing the spoons, which sound a bit like castanets. I love being in a group, making lots of noise. Everyone is jiving to the music. It fills the room.

Myrtle gives words to the tunes the jazz band have been playing all term, without a singer. 'Won't you give me Doctor Jazz', 'Nobody Knows You When You're Down and Out' and 'Careless Love'. Sometimes when she sings on her own, she plays a zither or autoharp with lots of strings, hugging it against her like a recalcitrant baby. *'Fal de rall de day.'*

English folk songs, or ballads, are too shouty for my taste. Myrtle hasn't got a pretty voice. She's loud and strident, but I admire her showmanship, her bravado.

Evie doesn't play an instrument, but she can dance. The two of us are jiving energetically to the music and then we break off. Evie does her own lovely dance across the floor, showing off to her mother, but Myrtle ignores her. It's as if Evie isn't there. Myrtle is too busy chatting to my little brother, giving him cigarettes. Chrissy cuddles up to Myrtle, with Evie sitting on the other side of the

room, picking at the floor. I wonder how she feels about this?
She never says.

In the school holidays we get farmed out as paying guests. Sometimes my brother Chrissy and I go to the same people. Sometimes
we stay at the empty school as if we are ghosts, haunting an
abandoned community. No one seems to like the holidays. Some
parents, the absent ones we had all been hearing about in the dark
after lights-out, suddenly arrive to pick up their kids. We go to the
station to see the others off, the ones flying back to their homes in
America. There are tears and hugs. It seems like no one wants to
go home. I wish I could be like them, to have a home I don't want
to go back to. It's the only time I'm properly aware of a difference,
something missing in my life.

Sometimes I join the Brights on trips to London. We go to the
King's Road where Julie Felix, a family friend, lives and we hang out
with Leonard Cohen's girlfriend, Marianne, a pretty Scandinavian
blonde. It's lovely being in a real flat with carpets and gas fires. I'm
not aware of the glamour. It's the comfort that impresses me.

Neill and Ena's teenage daughter, Zoë, goes to America for a
few weeks to join her boyfriend, Bill, who is teaching at a new
school, modelled on Summerhill lines. They've invited me to stay
in their cottage, up the path, at the edge of the school grounds.
Ena spoils me. There are carpets and armchairs, a television and
a gas fire; there is even a longhaired purring cat to sleep on my
(Zoë's) bed. The food is lavish, a stark contrast to the food I've

been eating at school. I feast on enormous scones at teatime, with clotted cream, and cut-glass dishes of strawberry jam, shepherd's pie, apple crumbles, with cream again, and all the biscuits I can eat.

Neill is a detached presence. He is mostly at the school in his office during the day. In the evenings, he sits in his armchair smoking his pipe, with Biscuit at his feet, watching the news. I never knew my grandfathers. With ears as big as a baby elephant's and hairs sprouting all over the place, his big veiny nose and his wrinkled, turkey neck, Neill is the only old man I know. The pipe, the accent, his huge feet in shiny black lace-ups: he might as well be an alien from another planet.

Ena is attentive, kind in her own brusque way. We do a lot of baking. We even make shortbread with Ena showing me how. I make a box of it up and send it to Uncle Tom back in New York. Sometimes I feel sick with the amount I've eaten. I sense that this is a short-lived thing, and I better make the most of it while I can. Of course, when Zoë returns, I'm sent back to my own room in the empty school.

Chrissy and I drift from family to family. Chrissy is volatile and emotional; I am shy and tearful. I like to stay in my room and read a lot. We stay in a thatched cottage in Sussex. Radio 3 is broadcast from morning until night; there's an Aga, cats, and an elderly spinster who's a retired teacher. There is something sexless, almost deathly about it all, the misery of Radio 3. I hate it there.

What a relief, then, to fetch up at the farm in Hertfordshire with Nanesse, a slim and elegant Scots woman with a sarcastic wit. She sends us out for enforced walks.

'Children must have exercise,' she says.

I hang around, as close to the house as possible.

'Mikey's afraid the house is going to run away without her,' says Nanesse.

She isn't wrong. I *am* afraid. I just want to stay in my room where I'm safe, reading a book or playing my guitar.

The house is an old mill on a farm that is so ancient it has a watchtower from a thousand years ago. The mill has an untended garden filled with stinging nettles and hissing geese that charge at you if you venture into their territory. The never-ending sound of gushing water greets you as soon as you open the back door. Beyond the nettles there's a wood with tall spindly trees: rooks' nests pronged onto black branches – the rooks' harsh cries hacking at the grey and endless sky – and beyond the wood, wide flat fields of yellow grain in summer, burnt to stubble in the winter. Straight roads, built by the Romans, run alongside the fields of wheat.

In the summer, we are sent outside to hang around, and climb the only tree that grows by the side of the grain field, or play in the hay bales. At teatime, we are allowed to take a striped plastic beaker of fluorescent orange squash and two biscuits – a custard cream and a bourbon.

Nanesse has two little boys, James and Fergus, and a dog, Fingel, a slobbering brown boxer. James is being potty trained, and when he goes to the loo, he shouts, 'Bend down on the launcher,' a cue for Nanesse to come and wipe his bottom. There is a fluffy patchwork cat called Shadow who I rescue as a kitten (the runt of a litter) and nurse over the summer holidays. There is a husband too, who works nights at Reuters. Nanesse is a great cook. The kitchen has an old, cream-coloured Aga, with a wooden drying rack hanging from the ceiling. The kitchen is where I most want to be, but Nanesse won't let me in when she's cooking.

To my enquiry, 'What's for dinner?' Nanesse always replies, 'Poison.'

The Aga burns an unsatisfactory coke, not heavy and oily like coal, but porous and grey. When my periods come I have to carry my sanitary towel, wrapped in loo roll, to the stove, lift one of the round metal doors at the top with a metal prong, and throw it inside. I wait in the loo for a moment until the coast is clear, run to the kitchen and fling it into the inferno.

It is always odd, being suddenly in a domestic space. It takes a bit of getting used to.

Nanesse is an accomplished dressmaker with a more sympathetic eye towards quality and style than Ulla. We go to Hitchin market every week, choosing the fabric for, say, a poncho, or even a suit; tartans (vegetable dyed, of course), fabulous Donegal tweeds. A length of sage green linen is made into a shift dress to which Nanesse adds an antique lace collar from her sewing box. My poncho (hooded) is lined in comforting dark-green needlecord. Nanesse uses all the latest patterns from *Vogue* and Butterick. Ulla has only old patterns, torn and mended with Sellotape, which have to be adapted and re-used.

I revel in the attention, the journey to Hitchin, walking around the stalls with Nanesse and touching the fabrics. I follow her example, feeling them for their quality, the cottons, lawns and glazed chintzes, the nylons and synthetics; the tartans, tweeds, paisley, patterns and stripes, printed or woven, and the planning and cutting out to look forward to. Being twirled and pinned. All of Nanesse's kindness goes into this activity; this is how she loves, and it's easy for me to receive.

A German boy called Hans comes to stay. He is seventeen or eighteen, but he seems like a man to me – tall, blond, handsome and terribly polite. He asks me lots of questions and seems to be interested in my answers. No one has treated me with such deference before. At night in bed, I arrange my hair across the pillow, dramatically, with the door ajar in the hope that Hans when he walks past on his way to bed, will see me as a sleeping beauty (although I am wide awake); perhaps he will be so overwhelmed that he will come into my room and – what?

Kiss me?

But Hans is decent and gentlemanly, at least he is with me. When Jemima arrives, flirting and giggling, they cavort and chase each other around the bedraggled garden.

'Oh Hans, you're tickling me, stop!'

I'm mortified.

Why can't Hans see the woman I am inside? I'm thirteen and

a half, but to him I'm only a child. I am hopeful when he asks for my address at Summerhill, but it's only so his little sister, Brigitte, can write to me.

'You can become, how you say, pen pals. Swap informations about your life. I think you would like my sister. You are same age, and she is very shy like you. She would like to be practising her English.'

Brigitte and I do write to each other, for a long time, formal letters about our lives. We send each other singles. I send her The Small Faces, singing 'Itchycoo Park', and she sends me a record by Michel Polnareff, a French heart-throb who sings something called 'Love Me, Please Love Me'. She sends a poster of another heart-throb called Adamo: a sombre looking boy, with long wavy, dark hair. I'm not impressed, but I put the poster on my wall anyway.

Christmas holidays are coming up, and I'm sitting on Anna's bed. She is folding her clothes and putting them carefully into a suitcase, looking forward to Christmas in California with her family. I'm looking forward to seeing Nanesse, to the house and it's domestic comforts.

'I wonder how Shadow, my kitten's, doing?'

'Probably not a kitten anymore, I guess.'

'Oh yeah, she'll be fully grown. I wonder if she'll recognize me?'

'There's a coat I really want to make. I haven't got the pattern or the material yet, but Nanesse will help me. She's so good at making things. And the food, it's delicious.'

Instead, at the last minute, we go to Sussex to stay with Jean, the spiteful old witch who listens to Radio 3. Nanesse has scandalized everyone, even Neill, by having an affair with a very mature-looking fifteen-year-old American boy, who had been staying there at the end of the summer holidays. Nanesse had written him passionate poems, which her husband has found. We never see or hear from Nanesse again.

I hide my broken heart.

There is no sewing at the witch's house so I spend my time making a mosaic picture from tiny bits of coloured paper, cut out from the Sunday supplements. It's of a lady playing the guitar.

Sean, for some reason, usually stays with a blacksmith's family down in Brighton, who are actually called the Blacks. After his first holiday he comes back with a hipster belt he has made. It weighs about a stone and has several metal rectangles linked together with double chains, fastened with spirals of metal at the front. He looks very fetching in it, clasped around his thin hips, with his velvet flares. Later, aged fifteen, he is badly beaten up in a mod and rocker fight on the beach (no one seems sure whether he was a mod or a rocker). At any rate, a very big man hits him over the head with a spade, and he's in a coma for a week.

When he wakes up, he says, 'I'm very hungry.'

Apart from that, he seems to be unscathed. The man who hit him is tried and gets sent down for ten years.

Chapter 16

A new maths teacher has arrived. His name is Paul and he's fleeing some emotional scandal at Kilquhanity. He is a handsome silver-haired man who is fond of a drink or two. In the summer he sits outside the maths hut at a rickety old table, bare-chested, playing cards with his pupils, which is as good as any maths lesson, he says. Ulla and Margaret, another housemother, years younger and more cynical than her German counterpart, vie for his attention. There are rumours that they've been racing each other to Paul's hut with cups of tea for him in the morning, just before the breakfast bell.

I can't imagine Ulla being in love. She's much too old for all that, too set in her ways. Perhaps when she was young and had her hair in that long plait.

Predictably, Paul with his taste for beer and roguish charm, manages to wreak havoc throughout the staff cohort. He is said by Neill to be 'in his cups' (drunk) once too often. When this happens, he is argumentative, critical of the school to anyone who cares to listen.

He manages to divide the staff by getting some to side with him. Paul seems to have the measure of Myles, and even dares to suggest that Neill should sack his stepson. Above all, he is abusive to Ena, shouting that he won't be ruled by 'a petticoat government', when she tells him off for a misdemeanour, invariably involving food or crockery.

I am alone with Ulla in her room one evening, helping her with some wool, holding a skein of it in my outstretched hands, while she winds it expertly into a ball. When she has finished, she puts her head in her hands.

'*Ach, mein Herzchen*, you will understand when you are older, what it is to have your heart broken. Your Ulla is an old fool, I know, but she cannot help it. I would do anything for that man, and what does he do, but turn his attentions to that Margaret woman. She doesn't care for him as I do. She will have her fun and then tire of him. I don't expect you to understand how I feel. I just need to speak of this or I will burst with grief.'

I'm patting her grown-up back with my child's hand (*there, there*), but her heartbreak and her tears strike me as comical, disturbing. It doesn't suit my image of Ulla at all. She's right. These are emotions that I can't understand. I am numb and can offer her no comfort.

Paul doesn't wait for Neill to sack him. He resigns, and heads off at the end of the summer term to teach at a new school in America, another copycat, run on the same principles as Summerhill.

The young, sparkly teachers never stay. The isolation and poor pay isn't a long-term prospect for anyone with ambition, or a life to lead.

'*Spaseeba Tovarich*,' Vicky and I say to each other when we are being polite.

'*Zdrazvooteay* and *Dazveedanya*,' when we say hello or goodbye.

A twenty-two-year-old Russian graduate from America comes as a housemother, and begins teaching a group of us Russian in her spare time. She has been studying in Moscow and then Paris. She has a continental elegance, beautiful shoes, slim suntanned legs, her fuzzy hair in a chic French roll. We learn the Cyrillic alphabet and then some dialogue.

I can write in Russian: *Ya tebya lyobloo* (I love you).

But Jane doesn't return the following autumn.

We miss her.

No more Russian.

Randy and Lewis arrive, a gay couple from California, to teach kindergarten. The children adore them, but Neill disapproves of their teaching methods. Montessori is not Neill's thing at all, not to mention their homosexuality, which Neill is sure he could cure if they would only let him try. At heart he's a Victorian and mistrusts all that learning through play. You either learn in a classroom, or you play. You don't mix the two. Neill lets them go after a term.

After my disastrous pairing with Jemima Ena finally gives me my own room, downstairs at the back of the house, near the kitchen and the back door. Small and high ceilinged, there is enough room for a single bed with Mimmy's blanket, a chest of drawers and a desk under the window. Everything I own is here. My guitar, my record player, my clothes, my books, the wooden tuck box my little brother made for me in woodwork, painted glossy red, and with a padlock.

In the corner of my room is the wardrobe I've made in wood-work class. Well, it only needs one side, and there's a wooden pole with brass fixings to attach it. I make an orange curtain in Ulla's room to hang over the front. There are wind chimes at the window, magenta, yellow and orange, made from semi-translucent, rounded shell. The colours, faded in the sun, make a lovely noise. One of the older girls, who is quiet and serious, has made me a multicoloured felt bird of paradise, which hangs on a thread at the window too. There's an attractive poster from Scandinavia, with *Aarhus Festuge* on it, and a poster of Bob Dylan wearing a corduroy peaked hat. My record player and small collection of singles and EPs are in the corner.

My room is by the back door. People call by at nights when they can't sleep. My light is always on as I am still afraid of the dark. I'm usually reading or just dozing. Adam comes up from the carriages a minute after midnight on the fourteenth of February to make me his Valentine, but we are only playing. One of my English teachers comes in one night. I hear her outside in the corridor, crying. I feel inadequate with my comforting skills, but I try, I try.

I sit in my room with Millie for hours, writing ridiculous stories together, about vegetables, which she reads out loud in her strong Brooklyn accent, and makes me laugh.

> *Poor Penny, she was the only tomato left on the vine. There wasn't a single tomato left for her to talk to in the vegetable patch. She missed her friends who had all ripened before her, and been picked by the farmer, Owen MacRadish. One by one, the other tomatoes had left, even her best friend, Nogood Boyo, had gone. He'd been picked just that morning. But Penny was still a little green around the edges, and would have to wait her turn...*

When I'm alone I take out my collection of Polaroids and examine them, searching for clues. My mother is defined by two opposing seasons, winter and summer.

In the summer photo we're on holiday. It's the fourth of July in the Hamptons. There is a pier with, 'STOP all motors until boat is tied', painted on a sign in the background. I must be three years old, wearing a delicate white crumpled summer dress, stained with ice cream. I am looking down at it with trepidation, one hand reaching out to my mother. Mom, on the other hand is all poise, excited-looking, giving her attention to the camera, the photographer, while holding my hand firmly. She is wearing a beach creation, a halter neck dress (in reality a bathing suit with a matching ballerina skirt hooked deftly over it, turning it into a dress), and her favourite costume jewellery: monster-sized beads, one on each ear, with a group of them around her neck. She looks happy.

The winter photograph was taken a year later at the farmhouse.

Mom is standing in the snow, wearing a fur coat that seems to be weighing her down, squinting in the glare of all the whiteness, unsmiling for once. A neat path has been dug, cutting through the two feet of snow on either side, leading up to the house. Larry has written on the back of the photo, *'The blizzard of '56'*.

There are no children, no snowmen, because the children aren't there. We are with our father who has won custody of us because of our mother's drinking and unreliability.

Chapter 17

Uncle Tom is coming to visit. It's three years since we last saw him. We head up to Scotland to join Bob, Sean and Deedee, and catch a plane to the Isle of Islay, sheep scattering from the runway as we land. We go for lots of long walks, and visit whisky distilleries. My uncle is fond of whisky. We huddle together in the hotel bar, and the bedrooms, talking non-stop with wistful smiles, the thrill of names and events, stored away all this time, recognized at long last.

'Remember when Mom threw Larry's birthday cake at him?'

'Remember when Mom threw a watermelon through Larry's car windscreen?'

There seems to have been a lot of throwing.

Deedee fills me in and corrects me, reminding me of the details, names and dates. We live through the past we've shared, because we have no present together. Arguments break out as someone is accused or reminded of previous bad behaviour. These old stories or accusations will be brought out again and again over the coming years, to be aired and then buried, only to be brought out and renewed the next time we meet up.

Deedee: 'Hey Sean, remember when you fell out of the car that time, onto the freeway?'

Chrissy: 'Yeah, you held onto the handle for dear life until Mom stopped the car!'

Me: 'Sean's leg was in plaster, right up to his knee from that bike accident!'

Deedee: 'There were sparks coming off your cast while it scraped against the road!'

Sean is so accident-prone it's become part of his mythology. Other incidents include being shot in the finger with a BB gun and falling through thin ice on Great Neck Pond.

My sister and I share a room. It's bliss to be lying in bed in the dark, hearing her voice. I feel closer to my sister after our time apart. Deedee is nice to me; no teasing, no nail varnish on my face. I wonder if we would be talking like this if we were living all together like before?

'Deedee, why can't we go back?'

'Back where?'

'You know. *Home.*'

'I think there's still some kind of court case going on, and anyway home doesn't really exist anymore.'

'Well, there's Grandma's,' I say hopefully.

'Remember the doorman in his fancy uniform?'

'And the lift that opens right into the apartment, with Arthur there to greet us...'

And, just like that, we're back in Ten Eighty-Eight, as Grandma Cuddihy's apartment is known. You ride the elevator and the doors open directly into the apartment's black and white tiled entrance hall. You're greeted by the heavy scent of flowers, lilies, beeswax polish, the little stagnant pools of holy water at the feet of various Virgin Mary's, which stand at every junction and tabletop.

Here comes the infusion of Grandma's Chanel No. 5 and the soft, bustling movement of the Irish maid, there's a different one each year, or Violet (and later Henrietta), who does the cooking. Only the rustle of their uniforms can be heard, footsteps muffled by thick carpets, or rubber soles squeaking on the tiled floor.

'Do you remember Grandpa?' says Deedee.

'No.' I shake my head.

But I do remember the attentive older men, or 'uncles' who appear at cocktail hour, Martini glass clinking ice-cubes, to escort Grandma to dinner at Armando's, or the theatre. Otherwise they just hang out at the apartment, being served dinner by Arthur, my Grandmother's butler, who has been with my Grandmother for ever.

It's Arthur who comes to the telephone to speak to each of us in turn whenever we phone Grandma, usually at Christmas, staying with Bob. We stand in line by the telephone, in our dressing gowns, waiting our turn to speak.

'Is that you, Michael Elizabeth?'

'Yes.'

'Well, well, I'll be, if you don't sound just like an English lady!'

Arthur's accent is highly refined and enunciated, a little more quavery each year, with a nod towards Noel Coward.

'So, Michael Elizabeth. We hear you're getting to be quite an artist.'

And then my grandmother with her 'God bless you, dear' at the end of our brief conversation.

'Mikey…?'

I fall asleep before my sister has finished.

Chapter 18

I'm fourteen years old and, suddenly, our monochrome world erupts into technicolour. Suzanne with the violet eyes returns from California with brightly coloured pastels for me, colours I had only dreamed of. They make the powder paints in the art room look dowdy in comparison. Vicky and I buy men's collarless white shirts in a jumble sale and I dye mine magenta. No one has *seen* a colour like this before. The colour makes me fizzle with happiness.

The summer is baking hot. We stage water fights, soaking each other, running in and out of the building with bottles and jam jars. The tinies, led by Rebecca de Mornay, go nuts. They steal into the art room, take their clothes off, prise open the big tins of rubbish powder paint, and throw it over each other. Then they run outside, trailing rainbow footprints through the corridor, and roll around the grass in the hockey field. Their housemother has to hose them down outside which sends them into tickled fits of more laughter. They are brought up in the Friday Tribunal, and fined their pudding for a week.

*

On Sunday mornings we sleep in and go to Tufford's, just the other side of the railway tracks and the level crossing, for breakfast. All week I long for the luxurious hand-cut white bread, toasted, and oozing melted butter, washed down with cups of frothy coffee. I happily spend most of my pocket money here. If there is any money to spare, we put it in the jukebox. The local boys and Summerhill boys play the pinball machines, shaking and juddering the machines from side to side to help the pinball reach its target.

Men in flat caps, most of them on bicycles, spill out of the factory opposite after the wail of sirens announces the end of a working day. Some of the men are just lads, not much older than the boys at Summerhill. Sometimes these boys, or men, come into the café. The café is a social hub. The unpredictable music on the jukebox, the ping of the pinball machines, and above all, the possibility of an encounter with a male stranger – a look, a glance, an exchange of greeting – leaves me fluttery with excitement.

David Brown (I find out his name from my little brother) has a friend called Rob, tall, thin and gentle, who works in the factory. He likes me, so I hear, but I prefer Dave who seems sharper, more edgy and dangerous. He's a mod: he drives a scooter. He has a pretty boy's mouth, slightly bouffant hair and he wears an army green parka. I'm impressed. Too shy to approach him, I create romantic scenarios in my head. I write his name down, several times, and sleep with the paper under my pillow, and make significant connections in minor things; the numbers on a bus ticket, for instance, correspond to the number of letters in the alphabet: 4 = D, 2 = B (like Neill's algebra). I am obsessed, and amazed when my bits of witchcraft draw him to me.

One day, he comes to the school to find me. (My little brother tells me, many years later, that David promised to give him five Woodbines if he would introduce him to me, so he did.) David has a crash pad, a little hut by the level crossing, where we lie on old army blankets and make out, but I'm not ready or willing to have sex with him, not yet anyway. He certainly doesn't love me. He actually has a girlfriend already, a very pretty brunette with almond eyes, who I see in town sometimes, and anyway the surroundings, the shed and the blankets, are less than salubrious. But I let him kiss me, and once, he squeezes my right breast so hard it hurts.

When we go away for that week on Islay together with Uncle Tom, and I lie in bed with my sister in a shared hotel room, she tells me about losing her virginity in Paris, where she was working as an *au pair*. The older man had put a pillow under her back to make her more comfortable. How considerate. If I have sex with David Brown, I want it to be like that.

I'm relieved, in a way, when Neill calls me into his office where there's a lot of humming and hawing from him. His pipe produces a welcome smoke screen between us. One of the tinies must have been here for a PL: the family of naked rag dolls that Neill keeps for them to play with are jumbled up on the floor; the mother and father with their pubic hair, the boy and girl, all of them with their rag doll genitalia, probably made by Ulla a very long time ago.

'It's come to my attention,' says Neill between puffs on his pipe, 'that you've been seen with a lad from the town.'

I'm surprised he knows this much about me.

'Now, I don't object to this in principle, but apparently he's been spreading rumours that Summerhill girls are easy. I've no objection to sexual relations per se, in fact I'm all for it, but you are under age, and careless talk from outsiders, whether it's founded on fact or no (Neill says no rather than not), can seriously damage our reputation. The school could be closed down by the authorities if they get wind of anything untoward. We have to be very careful. Do ye understand where I'm heading here?'

He fixes me with a kindly stare.

'I gggguess so,' I reply feebly.

'I'm afraid I'm going to have to ask you to stop seeing this young man. It's for your own good, and the good of the whole school.'

It doesn't occur to me to disobey. After all, I have the responsibility for the whole school on my shoulders. I shed quite a few tears, but I'm secretly flattered that Neill has taken that much interest in my welfare.

Chapter 19

'*Naja*, I told you typies (Ulla's nickname for two or more of us), no more tapering jeans on my machine. Have you any idea of the cost of these needles? And anyway, your jeans are tight enough.'

Ulla, with pins in her mouth, is protesting my use of the sewing machine, again. She doesn't complain about putting a hem up for me. She's using a new-fangled machine that puffs spurts of French chalk. When she squeezes the rubber attachment, little clouds of chalk mark the hemline as I turn around. With Ulla helping me, I am realizing my dream. Like Scarlet in *Gone With the Wind*, I can fashion anything I want, luxurious and wonderful, from the most humble of materials.

Life, I've come to see, is punctuated by dresses, each one chosen and worn for a special occasion, and then discarded. Dresses conjure up a sense of nurturing affection. Homemade dresses (made with assistance) are proof of love, attention focused on me: turning tucking, pinning, darting. When I'm older, my first darts in a new dress make me feel proud to be acknowledged as a woman. Ena takes me to London during the Easter holidays – just the two of us. Centre Point has just been built, and we crane our necks, marvelling at its height, towering above us as we emerge from the underground at Tottenham Court Road. We stay in a little hotel in Bloomsbury, behind Heal's, where I buy some Finnish curtain material to make a dress with, bright colours which you can't buy anywhere else – fuchsias, oranges, reds. We go to John Lewis on Oxford Street, and Ena buys me a bra, black cotton, patterned with little pink flowers. I have been making do with hand-me-downs from Vicky, who is more developed than I am, so it is thrilling to have something new, and not Playtex.

We are sharing a hotel room with twin beds. It feels strange, seeing Ena in a long white nightie, her black and grey plait, which she wears in a bun around her head during the day, set free and dangling down her back. I feel shy and awkward from so much intimacy. We go to the cinema, to see a favourite film of Ena's, *Henry IV*, in black and white with Lawrence Olivier as Henry.

'It's a fleapit,' says Ena as we emerge from the cinema with bites on our ankles.

I make a dress from my material for the summer end of term party, empire line, with bell-bottom sleeves, and wooden buttons down the back. You can't beat a fresh pattern; slipping the flat, virgin sheets of tissue from the envelope and unfolding them. The tea-coloured paper, with the instructions: black lines, dashes, dots curves, numbers like road markings and intersections, tattooed into the flimsy paper. Cutting the pattern pieces out, being careful to cut along the printed black lines, and perhaps if I am being really fussy, ironing the pattern pieces flat, with a cool iron before pinning them onto the fabric.

The scissors cutting crisply through the layers of fabric make a satisfying whoosh sound. Tailor-tacking through marked areas on the pattern with double thread. Unpinning the paper, pinning the seams together and tacking, with a crude running stitch, and then sewing along the tacking with the machine. Ironing the seams and darts flat and then sewing the hooks and eyes; the buttonholes sometimes bound with fabric, or sewn with embroidery thread.

To go with my dress, I make dangly earrings from copper wire, with little pink and orange beads. Coming down the winding stairs into the lounge, my friends gasp and applaud. I love dressing up. We all do. It's a chance to shine, and I have spent hours, days, looking forward to it.

It's been a cold, rainy spring, but June looks promising, and the chestnut trees are in blossom. The Americans are talking about what they're going to do for the summer. I overhear them reminiscing about the sandy beaches in Malibu they've left behind, the surf, and the sunshine.

Ena approaches me in front of the building: 'Ah, Mikey, just the person I wanted to see. I've had a phone call from your Uncle Tom. He's sending air tickets for you and Chrissy, so you can fly to New York at the end of term, and spend some of your holiday with him.'

'Really? We're going back for a holiday? Are you sure? Did he really mean it?' (I almost want to hug Ena.)

I'm shocked, ecstatic, discombobulated. I run to tell my little brother, my friends, Vicky, Alex, Hannah, Evie, anyone in earshot. 'I'm going back, yes, back to America, for a holiday to see my family!' I wax lyrical about the beach. 'There's a hundred miles of beach, all the way from New York to the end of Long Island. There are sand dunes, and big waves, and the beach club, and great big jelly fish.'

With Ulla's help, I prepare outfits for the trip. My favourite dress has a psychedelic pattern and I buy a pair of quilted high heels in the same purple as part of the fabric to go with it. I make a trouser suit from blue-green needlecord, with a mandarin collar. A zip has to be ordered specially from London, a long one with a ring on the end of it to go down the front of the jacket. I make Chrissy another pair of trousers, and a shirt from an Indian bedspread, with a proper collar. This time it buttons down.

We talk about going *back* instead of going *home*.

'Ah, the English rose!'

Ten Eighty-Eight is just as I remember it with its shiny wooden surfaces, an enormous grand piano, photographs in silver frames, the crucifixes and statues of Our Lady. Henrietta, Grandma's maid, makes stacks of pancakes for us in the kitchen and pinches my cheeks:

'You eat up, now,' she says.

We spend a couple of days with Uncle Tom in the apartment he shares with his friends on West 86th Street. We go across town to see my Uncle Les. He and Tante Gabby live in the East 70s, not far from Grandma's apartment, with their two sons, Les III, and Henri. Their apartment and lifestyle couldn't be further from Grandma's. There are two bedrooms (the boys share), and large and wonderful meals are cooked on an outsized white enamel stove in a kitchen that hasn't been changed since the 1940s. They have a little dachshund called Dusty. I love it there. It feels curiously authentic, like a proper home.

Gabby tells me to, '*Asseyez-vous*,' and everyone's names are Frenchified.

We sit down for spaghetti and meatballs, my favourite.

'Your grandma saw the television show,' says Uncle Les. 'The film.'

'What film?'

'The conversation about happiness.'

I suddenly realize what he's talking about. Not a TV show but a documentary about Summerhill made by the Canadian Broadcasting Corporation. (It's not until I see the documentary many years later that I understand what Uncle Les is referring to, and the impact it's had on our lives.) It was made the summer of my magenta shirt and my newly grown hair. I'm practically a woman. I almost feel beautiful, and I'm loving the attention.

Neill is asked by the interviewer what his criteria for happiness is.

'I suppose it's just a feeling of balance, or well-being.' He pauses to chew on his pipe.

The off-camera interviewer then turns her attention to a long-haired teenage girl (Yes. It's me!)

'What do *you* think you get out of Summerhill that you don't get from an ordinary school?'

'I don't know,' I manage not to stutter. 'I just know that I'm here and I know I'm happy here, a lot happier than I was in America, and I know I wouldn't want to go anywhere else.'

I imagine Grandma Cuddihy watching the film on television in Montreal where she's visiting her eldest daughter, my Aunt Jane, and her seven grandchildren. Jane has a new television. Canadian TV has just gone over to colour. Grandma can't believe the change in me. How confident and pretty I seem.

'But, do you think it's doing you any good? The fact that you're happy here?' the interviewer presses the question.

'Yes, I think it is. It's made me not as afraid of things as I used to be. I used to be absolutely terrified of everything... I... I... I was just all nervous and tensed up and everything.'

'What kind of things were you afraid of?'

'I don't know. *Everything.*'

Grandma then catches a glimpse of Chrissy speaking in the school meeting. Suddenly she wants to see us. She's too frail to undertake the journey to England herself. Uncle Lester phones my Uncle Tom, they negotiate terms. Tom has no money. Grandma agrees to settle a substantial sum into his account, if he will promise to have her grandchildren flown over to New York to see her.

We drive out to Amagansett with Uncle Tom and one of his friends, a big friendly man with a deep voice, famous on radio and TV ads. My uncle drives with his arm around his friend, as if they're on a date. Chrissy and I sit in the back; the roof is down. We pass a familiar landmark from our childhood that shows we're nearing the Hamptons. It's a giant white duck, the size of a house, with a door on its front.

'Look, Chrissy, Long Island Duck Farm, remember?

The familiar smell of the duck farm wafts over us and we have to hold our noses.

Then there is the ocean and a wooden house on stilts. Aunt Joan is there with her curly-haired little girl, Wendy, and several of my uncle's friends, including Saul, Wendy's father. I think Joan is married to Saul now, but I'm not sure; she doesn't seem to live with my uncle anymore. We go to Southampton, where we lived those first few months with Uncle Tom, and I buy some knee-high, patent leather boots at Saks Fifth Avenue on Grandma's charge account. The shop is opposite the Presbyterian Church where I'd stood, six years earlier, waiting for Mom to come and get me. It doesn't register, so pleased am I with my boots.

Back in Manhattan, at Uncle Tom's apartment, I admire an old, Spanish guitar, which has been lying around the place. 'Tatay Valencia, 1861', it says on the tarnished gold label inside. I play something for him. It sounds much lovelier than the Korean guitar I've brought with me from England. Deep and resonant, it's so easy to play. Uncle Tom puts the guitar back in it's velvet-lined case and gives it to me. I leave the Korean one behind as an exchange. And that becomes the guitar I take down from the wall almost every day when I'm at home. (If Chrissy is jealous, he doesn't show it.)

I spend some time with my cousin Little Les or Les III, shortened sometimes to Third for yet more abbreviation. He is six years older than me, twenty-one, and studying architecture. A serious pedantic young man with glasses, he treats me with unaccustomed politeness, holding doors open for me, pulling my chair out from the table so I can sit down. He takes me to the Met, and talks about art. I feel special. When we part, he presents me with a book on the Impressionists, and a Rotring Rapidograph pen, which I take back to Summerhill and use to perfect my line drawings for the fashion page I'm writing for the school magazine.

Two years later, unable to convince him to contest his call up to Vietnam (I stammer a dwindling and unrehearsed argument on the telephone from my brother's flat in Edinburgh), I send Les III a little package of photos I have taken with my Instamatic, on my first ever trip to Paris: cherry trees in blossom set against a powder blue sky, some bronze nymphs in an elaborate fountain, and, after a little hesitation, Rodin's blackened bronze statues of sombre looking men. I imagine him lying on his bunk in Vietnam looking at the photos. Maybe even the Rodins look beautiful.

Coming back to England, at fifteen and a half, I have a sense of being grown up. More confident, stammering less, and I've lost the last bit of adolescent puppy fat. I've also grown to my full height of five foot ten. But more than that, something has settled within me. It's reassuring to know that *back home* still exists. It hasn't disappeared, but I've changed, I've moved on.

To what I'm not sure.

January 1968: I've come back to school early to take my O-level art. I have the art room all to myself: just me, Harry and a stopwatch. First I have to draw an old boot (one of Harry's muddy lace-ups), and then a hyacinth. This I manage very well, and later on – in the spring term when I'm studying for my other O-levels (a small group of us are doing English, history and French), Harry lets me know that I've passed with an 'A'. He seems quite pleased, and I'm practically carried around on people's shoulders: an O-level, and an 'A' at that! This is my first official endorsement that I might actually have some talent for art. And maybe, with Harry's quiet encouragement, it's the reason I decide to take it further.

In the Spring, my sister hitch-hikes down to Summerhill with her boyfriend, Charlie. They are both at art school in Glasgow. I give them my room and I share with Anna. I feel so proud of Deedee. She's my big sister and she's staying in my room, so glamorous. So different. Although most girls are wearing mini skirts, she's wearing a 1950s style circular skirt and ballet shoes. She looks like Audrey Hepburn in *Roman Holiday* with her long black hair tied back in a half ponytail, with va-va's (two buttons, round like balls, attached to rolled elastic, a French invention she has picked up in Paris, working as an au-pair). She is wearing a pair of large, hooped gypsy earrings, and for some reason, a wrinkled Colombo-style raincoat (this I find slightly disappointing). Best of all, she has her guitar with her, which she carries in a battered cream-coloured guitar case, dotted with stickers from all the countries she visited on a hitch-hiking holiday through Europe the previous summer.

When she takes out her guitar and sings, 'Mary Hamilton', I want to cry. Where our mother had been a high soprano, Deedee is a mezzo, or even contralto. Her voice rises gloriously. Sometimes she will burst into 'Summertime', or something from *West Side Story*. I join in but my voice trails away as I become the listener, arms awash with goose pimples, moved almost to tears at the sheer beauty of Deedee's voice.

'Deedee, you should *do* something with your voice. People would *love* you. You could be famous!'

'Thanks Mikey Pikey, but I can't be bothered. All those scales and practising and everything.' Deedee seems to have no vanity, no need for admiration. It is something she has always done effortlessly, so why should she value something that comes so easily? I know if I had her voice, I'd be up there on the stage like a shot.

A few weeks later, my sister writes to me from Glasgow. This time on heavy cartridge paper, torn from a sketchbook:

Dear Mikey,

I'm writing this in my freezing cold bedsit in Glasgow, sitting by a one-bar electric fire, with my coat on.

Charlie is coming over soon. We are going to see a movie, Bonnie and Clyde. *Charlie has agreed to go because there is some gun fighting and violence involved (we don't usually like the same movies). Thank you so much for lending Charlie and me your room; it was lovely, even the single bed was fine – a good excuse to really snuggle up. It was nice meeting Ena after all this time. There is something rather magnificent about her, but wow she's a bit of a battleaxe, isn't she? I wouldn't like to get on the wrong side of her; I bet she could hold her own against Grandpa Smiley. I'd like to see those two enter armed combat! I could hear her, shouting at the back door outside my/your room on our last morning at some poor kid who complained the milk was off.*

Ena aside, Summerhill reminded me a lot of Killy, and I felt quite homesick for the place. Neill reminded me a lot of John, expostulating in his kilt at the school meetings. But Chrissy seems to be an annoying little bastard – how many times was he brought up? How many fines was he given?

Art school is great. I really like making prints – lithography especially – but you have to lug these great big stones around; they are really heavy – I'm getting biceps! I'm making a whole series based around food and packaging. They are quite Pop Art looking – a bit Claes Oldenburg meets Jasper Johns (if you can imagine)!

*Bob seems in good form. I went over to Edinburgh to see him
last weekend; he's been organizing rallies, right left and centre
(well, mostly left!) on Vietnam… Charlie and I went to one of
them on the Mound outside the National Gallery. He doesn't even
need a megaphone, he's so effing loud! I don't think he plans to
go back to the US anytime soon, as given his previous sojourn at
Cardinal Farley's* (military academy) *he would be ripe for call up.
That said, everyone is worried Little Les will get his call up papers
soon. Of course his little brother Henri is exempt as he's at medical
school. Aunt Gabby is really worried.*

*Sean came up to Glasgow the other day for an audition at the
drama school. He did a monologue from Othello for the audition
(without blacking-up). He sounded very good, almost like Orson
Welles, but I kept wanting to burst out laughing at the final bit,
where he says 'I took by the throat the circumcized dog and smote
him thus' But Seanie looked so serious, so I didn't.*

*Still no word from Uncle Tom. I phoned Uncle Les, but no one
has seen hide nor hair of him, not since last summer when you
and Chrissy were there. Bob is convinced he's gone undercover
for the CIA. Where does he get that from? He has some idea that
adopting us was a cover for his covert activities; he keeps saying,
'Remember that trip he made to Angola?'*

*Bob says you are coming up to Edinburgh in September and
going to Napier to do your Highers – so you've finally decided?!
I hope you're not going to live with him. He will turn you into his
slave and make you do his washing, or worse, try and sell you to*

his friends – remember the last time you were in Edinburgh – that
'mature student' friend of his from South Africa who kept wanting
to take you for a drive up Arthur's Seat? Anyway, don't do it! (I
mean the living with Bob bit.) It will be great to have you living
in Scotland! Wow! That just leaves Chrissy – all on his own in
the land of the Sassenachs!

Oops – Charlie is knocking on my door – movie time!
Lurve and kisses,
Your big sister,
Deedee

PS Give Chrissy a hug from me! Tell him to stop bugging everyone,
and go to some lessons!

I want to *be* my sister so I double my efforts on the guitar but
I am afraid of my own voice. I let the guitar do the singing for me.
In order to emulate Deedee further, I make myself a circular skirt,
machining yards of bias binding to the hem. I prefer to hide behind
my hair, so I don't tie it back, like Deedee.

Ena confronts me, walking down the path to the school from
her cottage: 'You know, dear, you could be a very attractive young
lady if only you would put your hair back away from your face.'

It sounds like she's scolding me. She picks my hair up, a hunk
of it in either hand, and demonstrates how lovely I could look. The
unfamiliar draft on my face, on my neck is uncomfortable. I want
to stay hidden. This is the only compliment I will ever receive from
her, and I don't take her advice, at least not for the time being.

*

Sometime towards the end of my final term, Ena takes me on the train to London. We are going to somewhere called Harley Street where she tells me, I'm going to be fitted for a Dutch cap.

How can I tell her I'm still a virgin, that I don't need whatever it is she's offering me? I feel a mixture of shame and fear. Perhaps she will be disappointed in me if I tell her I'm not ready for this, that I'm not as grown up as she thinks I am. I'm reminded of the stockings Grandma sent me when I was ten years old, in their gift-wrapped box that were just too grown up for me. I am sure that Ena will be angry with me if I turn down her offer, this special treat she's prepared for me, so I remain silent.

We arrive at the doctor's, the gynecologist's; a shiny brass plaque with his name etched in authoritative letters on the front door. I am led into a consulting room, leaving Ena behind in reception, flicking through a copy of *The Lady*.

A grey-haired man stands up.

'Hello there. Now if you'd like to take your panties off, we can get started,' he says, rolling up his sleeves, and rubbing his hands together.

I am too awed by the experience, coming up to London, and the promise of shopping in Carnaby Street, to be frightened, and anyway, I really don't know what to expect. I lie on the bed with a sheet over my legs. He tells me to bend my knees, and look at the ceiling. Cold hands entrap me; one prods my tummy while, with the other, he puts what feels like his whole hand inside me.

The shock of penetration, never mind the pain, is overwhelming. (I have recently wasted a whole box of Tampax, trying in vain to make them 'work' so I don't have to wear a sanitary towel when I have my period.) Afterwards, he pulls a tissue from a box on his desk, tells me in an angry, dismissive voice, to dry my tears and clean myself off. Later, I am given a plastic compact, with a sweet smelling rubber dome inside it.

My legs feel shaky and unsteady as we walk away down Harley Street.

In an attempt to sound bright and breezy, Ena says: 'Now, you can keep that diaphragm in your handbag when you go to parties, just in case. Isn't that grand?'

'Mmm,' I murmur, trying to picture what kind of handbag that might be, as I don't actually own one.

Walking with my head down, I notice that little rivulets of blood have dried on my inner legs, stopping on the ledge of my ankles, as we make our way towards Oxford Street.

I just want to go home.

Chapter 20

My brother Bob is anxious to provide a home for us, in the holidays at least. It's increasingly obvious that Uncle Tom isn't up to it; it's almost impossible to reach him on the phone, and sometimes he just goes AWOL.

Bob befriends a family in Edinburgh, where he's gone to study for his Highers at Napier Polytechnic – the father, Donald, is a political activist whom he admires. Chrissy, Sean and I are invited to spend Christmas with the McKenzies and their two children. For some reason, I decide to decorate the white linen cloth on my bedside table, and I trace round and round an old penny with a biro, making a delightful pattern on the white. When Marion, the mother, discovers it the following day, she wants to know who could have done such a terrible thing. I don't own up, I feel so ashamed.

I receive a rare letter from Bob in Edinburgh – typed (the spaces in the o's and a's are clogged with typewriter ink:

Dear Mike and Chris,

I may not write often, but at least I try. Mike, I hope your present has reached you (a little book he's sent me on Matisse – my favourite artist). *I am sorry it is late, but I have been running about lately and really do not know if I am coming or going. I guess that is not unusual.*

We had a tremendous demonstration on the war in Vietnam. Five hundred people, which in Edinburgh is not bad at all, were on it. Flags, banners and 'Victory for the Viet Cong!' All in all, not bad. We are hoping to have a big meeting when Lawrence Daly comes back from North Viet Nam, but we are not sure.

I went for an interview at Sussex and to be honest, I did not really like the place. Edinburgh want me for politics, but there is a lot of guff about my not having such and such. I fear I will not get into Edinburgh. Well, Stratchclyde still has to let itself be known. I read the letter you sent to Donald and things sound super at Summerhill. I must say I am very happy about that. Keep it up. Christ I am an old reactionary aren't I?

Edinburgh is cold and wet tonight. Went to see a 'shoot em up' with Liz (Bob's girlfriend) *and we were nearly blown away. The President of Iceland, good old Iceland, went driving by for a banquet in the Castle. Liz, with her dislike of Milne's bar, wouldn't let me go and have a pint. Just what I need was a good pint.*

Now can you tell me if you want to spend your holiday with me? I assume you do, but would you please say 'yes' or 'go home' or whatever you want. There may be some confusion, but in a fortnight I should have things sort of worked out as far as holidays are concerned. Some of it may be spent in the country (Arran perhaps) but everything is up in the air. So a note on that.

And then in his barely legible scrawl:

Is there anything you need? I shall try and get it. Liz sends her love. Love Bob.
* there is a cottage I may be able to rent at High Corrie – very desolate.

Later, when Bob does get into Edinburgh University, he persuades a family on the Isle of Arran to take us on, hoping that the matriarch, Sheila, might be a good mother substitute for us. My brother is good at telling people our orphan story; he's good at drama. Sheila is big and fat and posh, but she has eight children, a small, skinny sculptor husband, and their house has recently burnt down, so we are all crammed into a little stone cottage halfway up a mountain, while her husband, some of her boy children and various student helpers, including Bob, get on with rebuilding the house at the bottom of the hill.

The other children have to take turns preparing porridge in the morning, and making the bread, several loaves of it a day. We spend a couple of holidays with them, in spite of it being a little crowded.

Eventually Bob begins to run out of friends who are sufficiently moved by his sob story to offer us accommodation, and he persuades Grandma Cuddihy to pay the rent on a big house in Morningside; big enough to accommodate my brothers Chrissy and Sean and myself during holidays; during the term time he fills it with his university friends.

Bob means well, but he doesn't have a father's protective instincts. He is always trying to pair me off with his friends, and Chrissy and Sean are antagonistic towards him, jealous and resentful at his self-appointed role as head of the family. Although he is the eldest, Sean and Chrissy just can't accept Bob's authority and I have to admit he can be a little pompous and overbearing.

Bob never finishes a meal, so busy is he talking, or smoking in between mouthfuls. He is afraid of silence – as if it will say too much. He never waits for a reply or riposte, he's happy with the sound of his own voice. Sometimes there's a brief hint of a stammer, a hesitation on his rat-a-tat-tat monologue about politics or a family story given mythical proportions. There's a story he likes to tell about when he was a baby, and a struggling young actor called Marlon Brando, who allegedly lived upstairs from my parents, used to push him in his pram. Every once in a while, he brings this one out and elaborates on it. Apparently my father electrified Marlon's bongo drums as well (maybe Bob means amplified). He speaks in a loud bark – never *sotto voce*.

Sometimes Bob picks on me:

'Mikey has had more dicks inside her than a police station.'

He addresses his comments to the room (there always has to be an audience), hoping for some laughter.

My sister and I roll our eyes in disgust.

'Bob, that was uncalled for,' Deedee says.

But I can see she's trying not to laugh, and I guess it is quite funny, although I wonder what kind of police station he's using as a measuring rod. Perhaps a very tiny one, on a small Scottish island, manned by two policemen, swapping shifts?

He hardly ever gives presents, but one Christmas I get a hand mirror that laughs hysterically when you pick it up.

There is a party at my brother's house.

My sister catches the bus from Glasgow with her boyfriend Charlie. She looks spectacular in a man's string vest worn as a dress. She's bra-less. She has a Twiggy-like chest, although that doesn't stop everyone from staring.

'That's fucking disgusting,' says the girlfriend of the university union rep.

The party is in full swing.

We are dancing to The Rolling Stones.

Suddenly the dancing stops. A fight is unfolding in the hallway.

Chrissy's voice: 'You fucking bastard; you're not my father. You can't tell me what to do!'

Bob: 'Yeah, well, who's gonna sort out all your legal stuff, and hold a pen for you so you can write your name, because you sure as hell can't!'

'Take that back!'

'Tell me, Christopher, when did you last read a book? CAN you even read?' My brother turns to the horrified party, grimacing in a particularly sadistic way.

'Take that back, you bastard!'

'Hey, Chrissy can't read!'

Sean: 'Steady on Bob, leave him alone!'

'Oh here comes Sean, all gallant all of a sudden; who do you think you are, Mr Clever pants? Ha! You can't even spell your own name!'

'That was just the one time, and anyway at least I'm not wasting my education. How much did Grandma pay to put you through military academy? And look at you, standing on your soapbox, preaching about Vietnam this, Vietnam that. You big phony!'

'Oh, that old chestnut. I wondered when you were going to bring that up again.'

'Why don't you go back to America and fight for your country? After all, you're the only one of us who's actually been trained to fight. But you're just a fucking coward. Chicken shit!'

'You fucking bastard!'

'You fucking bastard!'

'You fucking bastard!'

They are rolling around on the carpet like six-year-olds.

'Shouldn't they have grown out of this by now?' says Deedee.

Deedee is only eighteen months younger than Bob but she's his perfect sparring partner. I'm intrigued and slightly envious of their relationship, the banter back and forth, like a tennis match. She is unfazed by Bob, and I get the sense that he is ever so slightly afraid of her, or at least cares what she thinks of him. He is cautious with his insults. If he is too full on, she retaliates with righteous anger, and a lot of verbal feedback.

'Bob, I'm too old to be called an arsehole by you or anyone else, so back off.'

And he does.

When he turns twenty-one, Bob appoints himself our unofficial guardian. He writes a letter to Shirley Williams, the Labour MP for Hitchin, who takes up my brother's 'plight' – none of us have residence in this country, so it makes our status here precarious to say the least. Shirley Williams writes to Merlyn Rees, then in the Home Office, who gives my brother Leave to Remain. Due to the 'unusual circumstances of the family', Rees decides to count the rest of us as my brother's dependents, which means that any restrictions attached to our stay in Great Britain are cancelled, and we can come and go as we please.

We are no longer called 'aliens' as if we're from outer space. Now they can't send us 'home' on a whim although of course there is no such thing as *home*. Home is here, wherever we are.

We are staying in Edinburgh, in the house my brother Bob has rented in Comiston Drive since starting university. It's Easter. Uncle Tom has made a surprise visit. It's only the second time we've all been under the same roof since we left America. I'm sleeping in a little back bedroom with a single bed in it. I'm afraid of the dark so I keep my bedside light on. One night, the door creaks open.

It's not a ghost or an apparition. Oh my gosh, it's Uncle Tom, in boxer shorts, his chest covered in black hair.

'I'm scared', he says. 'Can I sleep with you?'

He doesn't wait for a reply. He slides into bed beside me. It's a little cramped to say the least. I lie there, holding on to the edge of the mattress, mortified, but pretty soon, Tom is snoring, out cold, so I get out of the bed and quietly get into his bed in the next room.

That summer Bob rents a big stone house on the Isle of Arran, and we all sail over to stay. Bob says I can bring a friend, so I invite Anna, who seems to have got rid of her cough. Several of Bob's friends come along too. He has started up a newspaper distributed throughout the Western Isles. Everyone helps printing, collating, stapling. There's an old army jeep, which Bob has decorated with a Vietcong flag.

Bob's girlfriend, Liz, rounded, fair-haired, Scottish and sensible, is the parent figure. She takes care of all the cooking and day-to-day things. Bob is like a big kid. It's Liz who will, over the coming years and decades, provide a home for all of us, even after my brother leaves her (when the children are small). It is always Liz and the children I come back to.

My sister has just returned from a visit to New York, where she managed to contact Uncle Tom.

'Uncle Tom's got so weird,' she says.

'How do you mean?'

Deedee was staying with Tom in the apartment he shares with his friends in the Upper West Side, or 'The Group' as he calls them. He gives her the choice of sleeping in his enormous bed with him, or down the hallway in a single, unmade bed in an absent flat-sharer's room.

'I'll sleep with you,' she says, trying to sound nonchalant.

That night, Tom turns over, and puts his arm around her, and tries to snuggle up.

My sister lifts his arm off. 'Tom, I'm your niece. *Back off!*'

'Gee, I'm sorry, Dee, didn't know where I was,' says my Uncle, sleepily, and he moves over to his side of the bed.

My sister tells me that Uncle Tom has married again.

'Really, who to?' I ask excitedly (picturing flowers, a celebration a honeymoon).

'Well, you know Tom and Joan got divorced so that she could marry Saul, the father of her little girl? (I nod, doubtfully.)

'Well, Uncle Tom married Maria, the nanny Joan hired to look after Wendy. She's from Puerto Rico, and the immigration people were going to deport her, because she didn't have the right papers. So Joan called in a favour from Tom. After all, she married him so he could adopt us.'

I imagine the bride and groom getting dressed in nice clothes to convince the authorities; Maria in a cream silk suit borrowed from Joan, with three-quarter length sleeves, a pair of white gloves, and maybe even a cute little hat decorated with net, and lily of the valley pinned across her heart. My uncle would be wearing his best

Brooks Brother's suit, a clean shirt and tie, hair slicked back.

Deedee says they made a fairly convincing couple apart from the quite notable twenty-year age difference. Maria is in her fifties. After the wedding, they shake hands and go their separate ways.

A telegram arrives from Uncle Tom; maybe he's announcing his imminent arrival!

PICKETED THE WHITE HOUSE ON VIETNAM FOR
ALL SIX OF US, LOVE TOMMY.

Ridiculously disappointed, I phone Deedee in Glasgow. I reverse the charges.

It's always Deedee we phone to complain about life, or each other. She calms us down, laughs at our jokes, and makes all of us feel we are in the right.

'Have you spoken to Uncle Tom recently?' I ask.

'No. He's *always* out,' says Deedee.

Whenever she tries to call Uncle Tom in New York, the telephone is answered by a man with a mechanical sounding voice.

'Who wants him?'

'It's Deedee, his niece.'

'He's out.'

Uncle Tom never comes to the phone. It's like he's fallen off the planet.

'Apparently the group of friends he's living with are into dating men and women,' Deedee tells me. 'All their kids live together under one roof in another apartment, and the grown-ups analyze each other.'

I don't know what to say.

'How do you know this?' I manage.

'I kind of figured it out.'

Chapter 21

It slowly dawns on me that attending Saturday's General Meeting is like facing up to a parent. We tell on each other, to the elected chairman and the room at large, and simmering feelings for each another bubble up to the surface.

Vicky's bossy sister, Kat, is chairman today. Nathan, who is taking the minutes, is sitting on the floor beside her, with his left arm around Evie. He is reading through the agenda in the ledger, his index finger tracing the lines of writing as he reads. The meeting is crowded with people slouching, sitting cross-legged, reclining. Rebecca is sitting next to Vicky, focusing on a piece of sewing made from felt, sewn with big fat baby stitches. Pete is standing with one of the tinies attached to his front, like a koala bear. Eleanor is knitting something complicated. Myles, standing in the shadows, is wearing dark glasses. Ulla is wearing a bright-yellow jumper, leaning against the wall halfway up the stairs, with her arms crossed behind her back; she's keen to get off as soon as she can and attend to some task or other.

'Millie and Barbara versus Adam, Jake and Chrissy for general annoyance,' Nathan reads out.

'Millie, tell us what happened,' says Kat, looking down at her.

Millie raises herself onto her knees. She's grown taller, less podgy, but still dressed as a beatnik in black jeans, black shirt, black-rimmed glasses. Her curly black hair, sticking out from her fringe, seems to fizzle with static. Barbara Ritvo (a blonde Millie lookalike) is hovering behind her with a smile of admiration and embarrassment on her lips.

'Well, they locked us in our room and wouldn't let us out, and they started flicking us with wet towels, and they wouldn't go away when we asked them!'

Adam is sitting on the stairs, resting against a banister, at the opposite side of the room from Millie. Braces are visible on his teeth as he smiles defiantly.

'Adam, do you have anything to say about *annoying* Millie?'

'Yes, I think it's stoopid!'

(Laughter from all present.)

'She's stupid, because she's always annoying us as well!'

Adam looks down at the floor, almost coquettishly, his pudding bowl haircut covering the upper half of his face.

'Millie?'

She gets up on her knees again, looking across the room at Adam.

'Well, I do annoy people, but I never really hurt you, and I don't carry it to extremes, Adam.'

'Ena?'

(With a smile) 'Millie, just think how *dull* your life would be if you didn't have these boys to annoy. What would you do?'

'Neill?'

(From his chair, dryly) 'I don't think the meeting has any right to interfere with a love affair.'

(Laughter all round.)

And so the meeting ends.

A shout goes up after lunch.

'Look, it's Leonard Cohen!'

I run to an upstairs window and look out to see a dark-haired man in a white suit strolling down the drive, shaded by the big chestnut trees, heavy with their pink flowers. And then, from a distant bedroom someone puts 'Suzanne' on their record player, at full volume, opening a window wide so the sound can accompany Leonard's tour of the grounds. Part of me feels a little embarrassed by the episode, but Leonard doesn't seem to mind. (Later, he sends his stepson, Marianne's son, to the school, a fretful little boy from Scandinavia, who cries a lot and soon leaves.) In the afternoon coaches pull up, full of Japanese tourists, all with cameras. Neill's book, *Summerhill*, has been published in Japan to great acclaim and, as a consequence, the school begins to fill up with even more visitors. The Japanese tourists outnumber us kids. They even come to our evening meeting, crowding us out, taking photographs, pointing and giggling behind cupped hands. The little kids show off, behaving badly. Everyone feels self-conscious.

A Special Meeting is called and a vote is taken on whether to ban visitors from the General Meetings altogether. After all, we argue, how can we conduct an honest, open discussion with a horde of strangers gaping at us as if we were monkeys in a zoo? Neill remonstrates with all of us.

'I want the visitors here. The Saturday General Meeting is at Summerhill's very heart and if they're not allowed to witness it, how can they hope to understand how self-government works in our little community?' says Neill.

We all of us, little and large, six years to sixty, raise our hands up to the sky, and vote against Neill. He storms out – the first and only time I ever see him angry.

Neill knows not to over-rule us; after all, he's set this whole thing up. This is his experiment and he has to run with it, whether he likes it or not. So, no more visitors, except under very special circumstances (if, for instance, a parent is visiting their child), and then they have to be voted in. This clause is added to the 'no visitors at meetings' ban when the issue is discussed a few weeks later at yet another meeting.

Late at night, Millie comes bursting into my bedroom, all excited:

'Oh my God, I just had sex with Adam. I just had to tell someone.'

'Wow, was it OK? Did you use protection?'

'No. But he didn't do it inside me, you know, ejaculating. I'll be OK, I have my period anyway. Oh my GOD, I just had SEX!'

Millie seems pretty happy about it all, and there are no reper-
cussions. She and Adam think of themselves as consenting adults.
My mind goes back to the incident, four years earlier, where Millie
was locked in the bathroom by my brother Sean. It seems such a
long time ago. Neither of us has ever mentioned it. Perhaps she's
forgotten all about it.

Every term, a committee of seven is formed to organize the end-
of-term party; to make the paintings and decorations that fill the
lounge. From half term onwards, a Saturday fair is organized every
week, after the General Meeting, with snacks sold for a profit; juice,
biscuits, and cream crackers spread with cheese spread. There are
games, homemade bagatelle machines (lots of rubber bands and
nails), and skittles. The money raised is used to buy the decorations
and food for the party. A theme for the party is chosen, the art
room taken over for the final two weeks and the windows covered
with newspaper. The room is locked with only the committee
allowed access. (We all keep the secret – it's imperative.) Those
who are good at art, or popular, or both, are voted on, and when
my artistic skills become apparent, I'm voted on every time. It's
almost like being popular. I love it.

The kids, ranging from thirteen and up, work by themselves
(Harry Herring opens up for us in the afternoons), creating wall-
sized paintings for the lounge. The walls are measured, pieces of
sugar paper glued together, and work carried on in great secrecy
in the art room. 'Op Art' has been a good theme. Jemima makes

an impressive Bridget Riley-inspired black and white patterned painting, with a Mary Quant-like model in the middle (hand on hip, Vidal Sassoon haircut). Evie, voted on because she's popular, paints something small. We work around the clock, the record player plugged into a light fitting dangling overhead.

What had probably once been an old carriage house is now the theatre. There are proper theatre seats covered in red velvet plush (a little the worse for wear) and a real stage, complete with curtains. The theatre, musty and cobwebbed, is opened after half term for rehearsals, swept of stray leaves and mouse droppings, the metal sheet (for thunder sounds) rediscovered, and rehearsals begin. Olly is the only adult who gets involved. She writes her own plays, and invites her favourites, mostly boys, to perform. They are quite good and revolve around a witch, Old Crock, played by herself. It's the only time she dresses in women's clothing, a long black skirt and pointy hat, leaning over a cauldron, and throwing sweets out to the children in the audience.

The rest of us always put on our own plays (a lot of the kids can't read) and musicals. I have a dressing-up box so I'm a good source of costumes. I write plays about wicked stepmothers so that I can get to wear Vicky's fake fur coat, and put my hair up. I also write a song with Vicky, 'I Wanna Be an Actress', which we sing as a duet:

> ME: *I wanna be an actress!*
> VICKY: *Actress?*

ME: *Yes!*

ME: *I wanna be an actress!*

VICKY: *Actress?*

ME: *Yes!*

ME: *I wanna have diamonds rings, extravagant things, fluffy furs, and chauffeurs…*

ME: *I wanna be an actress!*

VICKY: *Actress! But you can't act!*

On stage, I am another person. Everyone is patient, no one sniggers or teases me and, as if my magic, my stammer disappears. The Brights' parents, Marion and Steve have come to watch. It's thrilling to be watched by real actors.

I love the sound of the applause, and the laughter from everyone. We've made people laugh.

After the play's end, everyone rushes over to the main building, pushing through the lounge doors, which have been locked for a week, to be hopefully stunned by the spectacle that awaits them. The ceiling has been woven with a web of streamers, holding back a riot of balloons, engineered to fall down at midnight, the floor scattered with a liberal dusting of French chalk, to make the dancing slippery and more fun. It all looks amazing and unfamiliar.

I choreograph a dance routine – after all, this is our final party. We are tanned from all the swimming in the pool and at our most beautiful. Hannah (not Anna, who's too shy), Evie, Val, Suzanne and I paint ourselves gold, and dance, silhouetted, behind a sheet strung across the lounge, to a jazz instrumental version of 'A Hard Days Night' by the Ramsay Lewis Quartet. At the end, we burst through the sheet, naked (even me) and painted gold to a huge round of applause. Myrtle is there, with her band of merry men, and even she has to acknowledge Evie this time.

For our final leaving speech, Neill gathers everyone together under the balloons. The theme is Greek Myths and I've painted Orpheus and Eurydice (both blond, with Eurydice wearing an empire-line white dress), walking into the flames of Hades.

'Here we are at 1968,' begins Neill, 'and the world is a terrible place, full of pitfalls, and people who will misunderstand you.'

He chews on his pipe.

'We have quite a few of you older ones leaving this summer. It's going to be very different here without you, when the younger ones return in the autumn. Some might say that's a good thing (chuckle), but you've all made your mark in the community in one way or another, and I'm sad to see you go. Some of you will be going on to further education, A levels and the like. Good luck with that is all I can say! (Laughter.) To my mind, I would rather a lad chose to be a happy road sweeper than an unhappy professor. That goes for the lassies, too. Whatever your plans are, I hope that you have all gained enough self-knowledge and emotional maturity here at Summerhill to take you through the trials that will surely face you in that big wide world out there.'

He puffs on his pipe some more.

'You will come across people who may try to take advantage of you. Remember, they haven't experienced the freedom you have. You've been living amongst friends, amongst people of the same mindset as yourselves. You'll be entering a world where people are repressed, emotionally crippled, and taught to hate. Tread carefully. But I'm confident that if you face the world with honesty and love, you will get the same in return.'

Everyone gathers around the leavers in a circle to sing 'Auld Lang Syne'. We cry and hug, but I feel excited, looking forward to the life, with its pitfalls and dangers, that awaits me on the outside.

Part Two

Chapter 22

Edinburgh seems like the obvious place to move on to after Summerhill; my brother, Bob, is living there, and my sister is at art college in Glasgow. At first Neill and Ena send me to live with friends of theirs, who run an old folks' home on the outskirts of the city. But after a few weeks of mealtimes with the old folks I rebel and find myself a bedsit in the New Town, not far from my brother. It's in a Georgian crescent, in a flat with Chinese restaurant employees, for some reason. I run to the kitchen to heat, quickly, beans on toast, eating them shyly in my room, wondering at the goings on around me.

I start at Napier Polytechnic in September; it's an Indian summer and the leaves are still green on the trees. I love the Poly-technic – it's the complete antithesis of Summerhill. The building is completely new, all glass and metal, with a lift that goes round and round on a conveyer belt – you jump on and off it – and there are crowds of people, all new and unknown to me. I can't get over the novelty of sitting behind a desk and putting my hand up –

I love doing that; my stammer doesn't put me off. There are proper classrooms, with great facilities – earphones, tape recorders: '*Répétez après moi...*'

Mrs Macintosh, our French teacher, is strict, but funny – she wears tweed skirts and twinsets, which have a rather chic edge to them; the skirts are veering on sexy: not exactly tight, but just above the knee; the twinsets are beautiful colours: jade green, plum. I love the attention Mrs Macintosh gives me; she's censorious but encouraging at the same time.

There are real art classes, with a teacher called Kit Ferguson – in his corduroy jacket and tweed tie, he reminds me of the art teacher in *The Prime of Miss Jean Brodie*, which comes out in the cinema later that year, but without the bad reputation. Kit says my work shows promise – that I should go to art college and study painting. No one has ever said that to me before. At Summerhill, Harry Herring was merely on hand to unlock the art room, which was equipped with a meagre supply of powder paint, and poor quality grey paper. With Kit's encouragement, I start attending life-drawing classes in the evenings at the Art School to improve my drawing and build up my portfolio.

I meet Cameron, a golden curly-haired Marxist, in my second term. He's already at art college. He picks me out in a crowd of friends at the Café Royal, with its glittering, engraved mirrors, and circular mahogany bar. I go there on Saturday nights with my best friend, Shona, and others from the Polytechnic. We fill a bottle with a cocktail of spirits from Shona's father's drinks cabinet beforehand;

that way, with quick nips from time to time in the freezing cold ladies' loo with its art nouveau tiles, we can make half a pint of lager and lime last all night. Cameron is always surrounded by a coterie of admirers, mostly male, debating various aspects of society and modern thought.

Why did he pick me out? I'm pale and quiet with long dark hair. I guess he fancied I was some sort of Pre-Raphaelite muse to compliment his brilliance.

It's ages before we have sex. I can't seem to do it, to go 'the whole way', although I want to. At least I think I do. Perhaps it's my Dutch cap, that unwanted gift from Harley Street, that's putting me off. It's slippery, smelly and unwieldy, and I've never managed to use it, so we go to the Brook Advisory Centre for the pill. You have to be married or engaged, so I wear a cheap ring on my finger from Woolworth's.

By the time I start my second term at art college a year later, Cameron and I have set up home together in a basement flat in Henderson Row. We don't mind the mushrooms growing out of the walls at the back, or the toilet which is outside, across the basement well and under the pavement, or the fact that there is no bathroom. We wash at the sink – a cylindrical ascot to one side heats the water, which comes out in a boiling trickle from a thin metal pipe – which is positioned under the only window, looking out, to the toilet, and up, to the pavement just above our heads. Metal bars – railings – keep the passing legs of pedestrians, oblivious to the lives being lived below their feet, at a safe distance.

We make the flat look great; paint the stone floor in the kitchen bright blue, and a cast-off wooden table bright, glossy yellow. We scrub the wooden floor in the front room, and cover it with a Persian carpet – thrown out by someone in the street on 'bins night', and given a shampoo by me.

Chrissy, who is still at Summerhill, comes to visit in the school holidays with his best friend, Kurt, Joan Baez's godson; the two of them are inseparable. They look like brothers, with their long dark hair. I draw them both, hanging out in the flat, sitting on an old sofa draped with an Indian bedspread, or sitting on a variety of reclaimed chairs – Lloyd Loom and Eileen Gray. We listen to Cameron's Grundig stereo playing something by the Steve Miller Band, Captain Beefheart, or any number of American imports bought at Bruce's record shop in Rose Street. The red plastic carrier bag containing your purchase declares, in big black letters, *'I FOUND IT AT BRUCE'S'*.

Chrissy moves constantly, talking and smoking, looking this way and that, and I record his movements in my sketchpad, following them with my pencil. He gives me snippets of news about Summerhill; it's been over a year since I left, and I'm so busy with my new life that I hardly miss it. Why would I? Sometimes I miss the simplicity of it. I've had to learn cooking from scratch, and then there's the washing and ironing, and all the things associated with the outside world, like shopping, budgeting and paying bills.

Chrissy's time at Summerhill is coming to an end. Neill will give him his marching orders, just before his sixteenth birthday. A contributing factor could be that Chrissy's school fees haven't been paid for some time. Also, he spends most of his time in Leiston, with an older group of friends from the town, drinking under age at the Engineers Arms. Nevertheless, Chrissy is devastated when Neill calls him into his office to give him the news. He has started going to lessons, and he's even thinking about O levels. My brother Bob intervenes, and finds another school, in Ireland, but after a few weeks Chrissy runs away to London. It's the usual refrain: 'You're not my father, you can't tell me what to do!'

Sean comes to stay too – since he left Kilquhanity he's been doing odd jobs, staying with the Blacks in Brighton, sleeping on people's sofas. He's turned down a place at drama school, and the offer of a flatshare with my sister. He can't settle. He's been known to gamble a whole month's allowance from Grandma – put the whole £50 on a horse or a three-way, and lose it. Cameron and I go away on holiday, and he pawns my record collection (Joan, Jefferson Airplane, The Loving Spoonfull, Buffy Saint Marie).

'Sean, where are my records?'

'Gee. I don't know. Don't look at me.'

His denial of any wrongdoing is so credible that I almost believe it. There is no argument. He says he hasn't pawned my records, so he hasn't.

My friends and I go on forays to London from Edinburgh, taking the bus if we can afford it, but usually hitch-hiking; we leave after dark, and get a lift on a lorry, as far as the North Circular if we are lucky.

We stay with Myrtle in Notting Hill. I love walking down Portobello Road in the summer sunshine; so very different from my first visit, that Christmas of 1962. The houses, painted and decorated in frivolous pastel colours like enormous birthday cakes, and the streets lined with trees. Edinburgh seems grey and regimented in comparison: trees aren't allowed on the streets, but are fenced off in designated areas of green. Once, walking along Portobello Road on a Saturday, amongst the crowds, Joni Mitchell floats past me – petite and silvery blonde.

Biba is our first stop, the boots, suede and up to the knee in every colour imaginable, and matching T-shirts, with tiny self-covered buttons, trickling down the fronts, and tights, striped, to match. We walk among curly wooden coat trees, with coloured feather boas hanging from them, like exotic foliage. I can't afford much, but I always buy something if I can.

I never get over the thrill of being able to buy an item of clothing from a shop with my own money, but I always feel there is something shameful about buying a dress rather than making it. Even when I am earning my own money, it feels a bit like stealing, or like I don't quite deserve it. This guilt at instant gratification, does it come from Ulla, I wonder? I can just hear her:

'*Naja*, Mikey, that is all very well. You look very nice in this new garment, but the fabric is of poor quality. Look: 80 per cent synthetic – and the lining, so cheap – it will go into holes as soon as you look at it! And the price! It is five times what it would have cost to make!' And she looks at me, disapprovingly, over her half-moon glasses.

London is the place to be, I decide. After three years in Edinburgh – two of them at art college, I'm accepted onto the painting course at the Central School of Art. Cameron has been accepted for the illustration course at the Royal College. We move to London together. I'm nineteen.

Chapter 23

At art school in London, painting from the figure is on the way out. Most of my tutors are young, ambitious men who paint huge canvases, and use the latest acrylic paints from New York and yards of masking tape to make perfect divisions between one square or line of colour and another. However, the old guard, in the guise of a few bearded and wise old men, remain to teach life drawing and etching.

There are two life rooms – almost always empty, and with a model in each. The life rooms are lit from above by skylights, and there are wooden 'donkeys' (you sit astride them), leaning your drawing board between the ridges, across the front; they are very practical. The life room is my favourite place, and I bring clothes in for the 'girls' to wear, dress them up. Mary, a favourite – pale and Irish, with long dark red hair – wears my ivory-coloured kimono, patterned with flowers: red, yellow, black, gaping open, framing her bony figure. I draw her, using coloured pencils – a box of creamy textured Cumberlands; her skin is yellow, with purple shadows, and green.

And then there is Frances, black-haired, from Glasgow, who I draw resting – smoking a cigarette, wearing her own clothes: red patent-leather platform shoes and exaggeratedly flared jeans. Frances goes for teabreaks with me to Rosie's café on the ground floor, where tea is poured from an enormous metal teapot. When we finish our tea, Frances reads my tea leaves, swirling the teacup anti-clockwise, turning it upside down over the saucer before righting it, and examining its fascinating interior. These girls – I feel I know their bodies better than my own – every contour and shadow is familiar to me.

I draw our whole life in coloured pencils and crayons. I sit at the dinner table drawing our meals, the cutlery, the crockery; Cameron lying in the bath, now that we've moved to London and have a bath: 'Pink Penis nos 1–3'; Cameron reading; Cameron thinking; the armchairs – Lloyd Loom and Eileen Gray; Cameron drawing at his desk; my clothes; a patterned bedspread; my own legs and feet in the bath; a self-portrait; a sweetheart plant Cameron gives me for Valentine's day; objects laid out on a dressing table: brush, comb, mirror; a back view of my niece, Aimeé, as a two-year-old, in red Wellingtons and a pink dress, visiting with her mother from Edinburgh – a visual diary of our life together.

We're living in a little mews flat behind Wimpole Street that my brother Bob has found for me through his connections. The flat is owned by a philanthropic Labour peer, who charges a ridiculously low rent, and who parks his Rolls-Royce in the garage under-neath – the lease insists that 'no more than three young ladies' can reside there at any one time. There is a parquet floor scarred with little holes – the marks, I imagine, left from stiletto heels of debutantes, or high class call girls who have lived there before me. Christine Keeler lived next door but one during the Profumo affair in the sixties.

I don't appreciate the privilege of living in the middle of London like this until I start visiting my college friends who live further out, in Bounds Green, Acton and Colliers Wood. Soho – Berwick Street, where we go for vegetables and fruit on Saturdays – is just down the road. Speaker's Corner where we go on Sunday to listen to people debating is ten minutes in the other direction. College is just a bus ride, or a walk along Oxford Street.

Chrissy is living in Notting Hill now, with a girlfriend who is much older than him; she has two little boys. I visit him quite a lot. I love their flat, the little boys and Margaret's cooking, but Chrissy can be aggressive and confrontational. We both have a short fuse, so more often than not, his comments precipitate a slanging match, with tears and door slamming. He has no compunction (and remember, although he's six foot four, he *is* my little brother) about making judgements on my life and how I should conduct it.

'You know, sis, don't you think it's about time you stopped piss-ing around and got a *real* job? I mean, have you even sold a painting in the past year?' (Chrissy has had several jobs already, ranging from

Jamaica Pattie delivery boy to television cameraman to working as a navvy on the London Underground.)

'What? I have a part-time job. In fact, I have two jobs. I pay my way.'

'Yeah, but you're always complaining, going on about how broke you are. Why don't you paint something people want to buy?'

'If you think I'm going to put paintings up on the Bayswater Road railings, or sit in Leicester Square, drawing cartoons… I paint to survive, but not in the way YOU mean.'

'Don't be such a fucking snob.'

I've seen red now. There's no stopping me: 'Well, don't be such a fucking philistine. You don't know what you're talking about, so f-f-fuck off out of here.'

And he leaves my flat, or I leave his, and we don't speak for ages.

Cameron always seems to be lecturing me, trying to teach me – the right way to think, the right way to draw; my line is far too expressive for his liking – he never uses anything darker than an 'H' pencil himself. My line is wavy and fluid; his line is sharp and broken.

Now that we're at separate art schools, I begin to branch out and make my own friends. Perhaps inevitably, I fall hopelessly in love with someone else – a young man the same age as me. Our semi-affair drags on for over a year (holding hands surreptitiously in the park, followed, some months later, by daytime episodes back at his flat in Bounds Green.) Our desire is mutual – I give myself to him completely – but he has a girlfriend back home. He wants us both. His thinking is too sophisticated for me; I want him for myself. There are letters from him, written over a long summer holiday, from his home in the Lake District, on blue Basildon bond, several pages, folded thickly and crammed into inadequate, too small brown envelopes. I tear them in two in a moment of anger, and then carefully Sellotape them together again.

Returning to college for my second year, my resolve to have nothing to do with him crumbles as soon as I encounter him. He is tongue-tied when we meet, eloquent, always formal when he writes: 'Whilst we stood sort of awkwardly on the stairs...' It doesn't work out, but it creates some ugly scenes between Cameron and me. I move out of the mews flat for a while, until Cameron can find a place of his own.

I stay temporarily in a borrowed flat in Orange Street, W1, at the top of many flights of rickety stairs. The building is owned by an ancient old woman who has a club on the ground floor – a remnant from wartime called Jack's Club, which still seems to have customers, late at night. The flats are run down, decrepit; there's one very cold bathroom, which is off the kitchen, and shared by everyone. But it has a shabby kind of glamour, with its view of Nelson's Column from the kitchen window, and the rent is something like £5 a week – cheap, even by 1973 standards.

I rarely see Sean. Sean with his long hair, mannish Adam's apple, his slim hips, elegantly clad in velvet flares, always so charming and disarmingly polite, door-holding, pulling out chairs for women, helping them on with their coats (women and girls love him).

Uncle Lester is worried about Sean and writes to Deedee:

Your brother, Sean is still drifting.

That phrase seems to resonate: Sean, drifting.
Les goes on.

When he registered for the draft at the consulate, he put Kilquhanity down as his school. Of course, now he's left, the draft board could register him as 'delinquent'. His draft number is quite high, which means he is unlikely to be called up in the near future, so I suggested he come over and work for a friend of mine in Alabama who has a turkey farm. Sean didn't seem that enthusiastic.

I don't think I would've been that keen either.

At twenty-one, Sean finally comes into his inheritance – the bit of money my mother left and Uncle Tom cleverly invested, which we all receive in due course. He buys a Mini, painted with a Union Jack on the roof, and takes a road trip to Scotland. He buys a Super 8 camera and his friend films him climbing onto a statue of Bonnie Prince Charlie at some Scottish border town, and pretending to get off with it.

Sean has a caring, sentimental side. He is always the first to announce a birth, a death or an illness in the family. It's Sean who discovers that my mother has no headstone on her grave (Larry, the cheapskate!) and does a whip-round and arranges for one to be made and installed by The Southampton Granite Co. Inc. thirteen years after my mother's death.

Sean visits Mimmy as she lies dying in a California nursing home. Deedee and I chip in to buy a ticket for him. For that short time Sean is the perfect grandson; he even enlists Uncle Lester's help in getting a better room for Mimmy. My sister says that although Sean always seems to be doing the 'wrong thing', he has a prevailing sense of justice, and actually manages to do the 'right thing' quite often.

There is always a girlfriend from back home. Phoebe, wafer thin, blonde and refined, is the daughter of a Republican senator. A lovely girl, she's one of two sisters who went to school with my sister, Nanny, and lived next door to her. Sean moves to London with her for a year. They bicker a lot. Phoebe sews and home-makes. Sean goes to the betting shop.

And then when that finishes, he meets Patsy back in Southampton, a beautiful, capable blonde from a huge and loving Polish Catholic family. Sean starts to get work painting and decorating houses for rich people. He's very good. He works on his own, methodically – he's a perfectionist, always does a beautiful job. He is never out of work. Sean and Pat have a quick wedding at the Polish Catholic Church.

I don't think there was time to invite my sister and me, or Bob, but we send presents. Sean (well, Pat) sends photos of Sean wearing a powder blue, double-breasted polyester suit with huge lapels. Pat, in cream satin, has her little girl from a previous relationship, as a bridesmaid.

Chapter 24

Easter, 1974: I've just found out I've been accepted for an MA at Chelsea College of Art. I decide to fly to New York. It's Grandma Cuddihy's 76th birthday. Travelling from London in the grip of an early heat wave, I arrive in Manhattan in the middle of a blizzard. I take a taxi to Ten Eighty-Eight. The driver is spouting paranoia and guns as he points to the glove compartment, which he claims holds his weapon. (I'm reminded of him when I watch Robert de Niro in *Taxi Driver* three years later.) When I arrive, Uncle Lester is waiting outside in front of the canopied entrance, proffering a huge umbrella.

'I want twenty flat, and no arguments,' says the driver to my uncle as he rolls down the window.

All the Manhattan family are here, except for Uncle Tom. Uncle Les has hired a detective to try and track him down, but so far, he hasn't had any luck. Uncle Tom's absence hangs in the air, but that's how it is, how it's been for the past four or five years.

Everyone is polite. It's not a frosty English politeness, more of a kind interest. Here, everyone dresses for dinner. The men change into jackets and ties, out of consideration more than snobbery. They are gentle people. At Summerhill, everyone speaks their minds, but no one seems to listen. Here, my family seem to be genuinely interested in me. It makes me feel loved, important.

Grandma is sitting in her wheelchair like a shaky little bird; her beautiful platinum hair like a baby doll's. She's wearing a favourite dress by Junior Sophisticates (a line designed by Anne Klein for the petite woman). Her spindly legs are clad in the sheerest of stockings and the quilted leather shoes on her tiny feet are fastened with little gold buckles. She looks up at me with her lopsided smile. It's the best that she can muster. She is too small and fragile looking to hug. She might break but there's a core of strength there. I can see it in her eyes. She's not fragile at all; she's just not in full working order.

I've missed the party, so Lester makes me scrambled eggs on toast and I sit there, eating, after Grandma has been wheeled off to bed by her nurse, with my aunts and uncles in a circle, firing questions at me.

'So, how is life in London, England, Michael Elizabeth? You must be doing very well in your studies, being accepted for a Master's degree.'

'Do you see your brother Chris very often? How about Robbie and Deedee and Sean?'

My Aunt Jane wants to know if I have a 'beau' (a thrillingly old-fashioned sounding word), and I tell her that I do indeed (have a beau). I've been in love and out of love a few times since I parted from Cameron. Nothing seems to last, but there always seems to be something or someone else on the horizon – or at least the possibility of someone. You can almost hear me shouting 'NEXT' to whoever it might be, waiting there in the wings.

In the morning, at breakfast, I notice Arthur's hands are alarmingly shaky as he serves pancakes from a silver platter. Grandma raises an equally shaky fork to her mouth; I watch anxiously between the two of them, worried that each will miss their target.

Aunt Jane, or Auntie Cuckoo as she likes to refer to herself, is Grandma's eldest daughter. She lends me her Schiaparelli mink coat, and I traipse around the Guggenheim, the Metropolitan and other galleries, so gloriously nearby, in my ragged jeans, wearing the coat, a couple of sizes too small. Grandma sends me to Henry Bendell's and tells me to charge anything I want to her account. In a panic, I choose a pale blue cheesecloth evening dress, hand-stitched, by the designer Emmanuelle Khan.

Aunt Jane, a livelier and altogether funnier version of Grandma, wears the same lipstick and hairstyle, but she also sports a jewel-encrusted cigarette holder, with a menthol cigarette constantly on the go. She is despairing of my platform shoes. In London they seemed absolutely the thing, but in Manhattan their fashionable status is lost on my relatives. To them, the shoes look like a medical aid for a club-footed waif. Grandma and Aunt Jane give me a pitying look as they eye the shoes. As for my skirt, fashioned from a pair of old jeans, the least said the better.

Jane takes me shopping, to her favourite place, Encore Modes (second-hand designer clothes), on Madison Avenue, and I choose the least objectionable things, a wrap-around, knee skimming floral skirt, and for some forgotten reason, a one-shouldered striped T-shirt. I remain steadfast in my commitment to my shoes, however.

Aunt Jane is a Catholic in the best sense of the word. An ardent anti-abortionist, she is involved in a charity which takes young, expectant mothers over the border to Mexico – or is it the other way round – to have their babies secretly, and then adopted. She herself has seven children, the two youngest illegitimate. She refuses to marry the father who she refers to as 'Big Boy' as he is a divorcee, and not a Catholic.

Grandma has bought me a plane ticket so that I can visit Uncle Mike in Arizona. Although I'm looking forward to escaping the snow and ice in Manhattan, I am apprehensive.

I haven't seen Mike since before I went to Summerhill.

He meets me at the airport in Tucson with his wife, Mary. She had been his college sweetheart and they'd married twenty years later. Wearing a long, cheesecloth skirt, and a halter neck top, she looks a little like Joan Baez. Uncle Mike looks like an intellectual hippy, sitting there in his wheelchair, with his long hair and straggly beard, and a (necessary) leather band around his forehead attached to a metal rod down the back of his neck to keep his head supported and upright. He drinks through a glass straw. I have to lift it to his lips for him, and there is, of course, the famous rocking bed, to keep his lungs moving, and hourly sit downs with the oxygen tank.

I am overwhelmed by the landscape with its ridiculous, cartoon cactuses, and mountains springing up from nowhere like a whim of nature. The red land rolls past on a little visit I make over the border, on the bus to Nogales (the nearest Mexican town), bringing back trinkets, painted wooden toys, and a Tree of Life. Everyone has fragrant, civilized gardens, blessed with orange and lemon trees, in lush contrast to the stark, desert landscape.

Mike has an assistant called Bob, who dresses him and feeds him and attends to his correspondence. (Mary, apparently, refuses to be Mike's nurse because she wants to keep their relationship romantic.) Riding on the back of Bob's Harley Davidson, wearing the extravagant ankle-length dress from Henry Bendell's tucked up round my thighs, we head off to a party in the desert somewhere. I feel euphoric and free; why not swap my life for this? I could be happy here, un-stammering and brave, couldn't I? But it's just a fancy. The thought of changing my life, changing back to being American when I'm an English girl is impossible. London is where I belong.

Instead, I take whatever booty is being offered (an evening dress, a pair of fancy boots, a guitar). But it's the love I take away that nourishes me the most; it makes me feel light, giddy almost. When I leave to go back east, Mary puts a note in my case, which I find when I get back to New York.

Mikey, never forget that you are loved.

Back in England, I make some paintings from the photographs I've taken. The definition of the light and shadow is extraordinary. A pair of huge solid wooden gates are bleached grey from the sun. Clint Eastwood could ride through them on a horse, and not look out of place.

Chapter 25

It's the long hot summer of 1976, and I'm woken from a fitful, sweaty sleep at two in the morning, by the telephone. It's Uncle Les. Grandma has passed away, peacefully.

Later that day I phone my sister.

'Did you hear from Les?

'Yes.' She lets out a sigh.

'I wonder if Tom will show up for the funeral?'

'I don't think so somehow. Uncle Les says he didn't go and see her, even at the very end. He's not going to bother showing up to see her coffin.'

I can only imagine how Grandma would have felt. The absence of her favourite child, Uncle Tom, at her bedside must have hurt a lot.

Uncle Jack sells off the three largest and most important paintings from his collection, two Robert Motherwells and a Philip Guston, in order to buy the summer house, the Barn in Watermill, to keep it in the family. Jack and Heidi are left with some framed collages and drawings. In their Bank Street apartment the large, empty areas on the walls where the paintings used to hang will never be filled, their absence there for all to see.

The Barn (an ample five-bedroom house with a squash court) was once attached to a much larger mansion, built by my great grandfather, but Grandma gave the big house to the church, and they moved it somehow to another site. She was left with the Barn and a raised rectangle of grass where the pool had been. Returning to the house years later, I'm astonished by the squash court; I'd completely forgotten about it, but standing there, its damp smell and echo are so familiar, so recognizable, it throws me back to my childhood, and the summers I'd spent there with my brothers and sisters – as a family.

Uncle Lester completes an inventory of Grandma's affairs. The pages are bound together in a Manila-coloured folder, with a label stuck to the front, edged in red. He has made copies for each of us, and for my aunts and uncles. On the label, he has hand typed:

ESTATE OF JULIA MURRAY CUDDIHY

ACCOUNTING FOR PERSONAL PROPERTY

SETTLEMENT OF PERSONAL PROPERTY ACCOUNT

Inside, several pages in faded Xerox are stapled in on the left, itemizing her investments and the contents of the Park Avenue apartment, together with more valuable items of jewellery which were sold after she was moved to the care home during the final year of her illness.

On the right-hand side of the folder, are several pages itemizing the contents of the Barn; each room is listed with their contents:

BEDROOM 1

Pair colonial maple twin beds with bedding

Pair colonial maple 4-draw chests, small maple wall mirror

Yellow painted 2-tier dressing table with mirror top

Yellow painted cane-seat sidechair, yellow painted bench $50

Colonial-style maple rush-seat sidechair (poor condition) $20

Marble table lamp (cracked) $5

Floral upholstered chair (torn)   no value

Framed oil painting. Holy Family – in antique parcel gilt frame –
    Size 41' x 56' (condition poor) unsigned $300

My uncle has never had much interest in clothes. He is more at ease with listing the serial numbers and purchase dates of Grandma's portable radio ('*Sony portable radio. Model TFM 7100 W. AM/FM solid state., supersensitive. 11 transistors. Can be operated with 3 – 1.5 volt flashlight batteries. Bought by mother on 05/06/72*'), but he is determined to give every nightgown, slipper and dress its due. His description of each item of clothing seems touchingly poignant – a labour of love, although to a partial observer, his inventory probably verges on the forensic, or at the very least, obsessive.

I scan down through the pages.

Carton 2. Weight 19 Pounds.

1   sweater. Lined. 70 per cent lambswool. 20 per cent angora rabbit. 10 per cent nylon.

2   Jacket. Blue with white collar & blue buttons.

3   Dressing gown. Light green.

4   Dressing gown. Diamond pattern.

5   Dressing gown. Pink Bow. Floral pattern.

6   Dressing Gown. Pink with fringed bottom & sleeves.

7   Dressing Gown. Quilted with frills on front & sleeves.

8   Dressing Gown. White. Ornamental neck & sleeves. Elizabeth Arden.

9   Dressing Gown. Pink & white flower pattern & belt.

10 Dress. Sleeves with jacket. Black & white check pattern

11 Dress, sleeveless, Black & white reverse pattern.

12 Dress with sleeves. Zipper back. Large green flower pattern.

13 Dressing Gown. Flowered green silk-white lining. Elizabeth Arden.

14 Dress. Light blue. Zipper back. CHARLES LACOSTE. Alligator TM.

15 Afghan. Hand knit. 5' x 4' open work.

16 Pocket Book. small. Brass chain & leather handle.

Carton 3 10 ½ Pounds

1   Shawl. Pink, wool, small, floral pattern.

2   Shawl. White, wool, oval shaped.

3   Scarf. Green, fringed, mohair & wool.

4   Blanket, Pink, wool, fringed, 4' x 4', hand woven, orlon, arylic.

5   Lambs wool, 2 pieces. 30' x 30'.

6   Shawl, white, wool, 52" , wave pattern, fringed ends.

7   Pillow, baby's silk, with blue flower, ornamentation.

8   Bed Jacket, blue, quilted, lace collar, white lining.

9   Shoes. 2 pairs. 1 pr blue florsheim, black, white & red check buckles, low heels, size 5 ½. 1 pr white Joyce of California, sock lining, cushion film inner sole, U-shaped brass buckles…

It's exhaustive.

After my Grandmother's estate has been settled, my brothers, my sister and myself, receive a small settlement and a cut glass coaster each, with a silver rim, from a set of five (although there had once been six).

That's it.

Mine holds paper clips and small change, my sister's cigarette butts; my brother Bob's a whisky glass. I'm not sure what Sean and Chrissy's contain.

Chapter 26

Catching the bus along the King's Road, to the College annex, I watch out for the shop that spells 'SEX' in pink, padded letters. If the weather is good, Jordan (the original one) with her peroxide beehive and ripped fishnets, can be seen lolling outside, sunning her pale, pancaked face. Pretty is going out of fashion and my long hair, cheesecloth and espadrilles are beginning to look a little passé.

The MA studios at Chelsea College of Art are in a disused primary school past World's End. There are two of us to each huge, abandoned classroom, complete with blackout curtains from the war. There aren't more than twelve of us on the course, only two other girls, both girlfriends of blokes on the course (who are doing a second year). They dress like the boys in unflattering jeans and monkey-boots, no make up. They chain smoke their own roll-ups like the boys.

After graduation a group of us move our studios to a derelict warehouse in Bermondsey, which we occupy for a few years, until it burns down. The rent is barely nothing a week. Terence Conran lives there now. The wharf in Bermondsey, just over Tower Bridge, smells of cinnamon and nutmeg as if they have only just been emptied of their contents, and the sweet, heady smell of hops from the brewery further along. Between the four of us, we have a whole floor, dark, low ceilinged, with a wooden ramp at the front that hangs by big chains, double doors opening out to it. Fog rolls in from the river sometimes. On fine days, we sit there on old office chairs, salvaged from the wharf outside, and watch the river go by. We memorize the commentary from the passing boats, filled with tourists, and then repeat it to each other long after the boats have turned around and gone back.

I bring some of the skills I learnt from Ulla to my painting. I haul my treadle sewing machine to the studio, cutting into big widths of calico, pinning, sewing, stretching the fabric over a wooden stretcher, bigger than I am. I talk about 'making' paintings instead of painting them. By the end of the year, I've got my first show in a proper gallery, and a grant from the Arts Council. The following year a painting is accepted for The John Moores in Liverpool.

The painters in our studio are a conventional lot, coming in late morning, and leaving at a reasonable time in the evening to go home and cook dinner. There are others – performance artists, filmmakers, sculptors – who brave the primitive conditions, and stay around the clock.

Derek Jarman is making a film on the floor above us. For a while, I think he is making paintings up there, like me. It isn't until much later that I realize he is making a film called *Jubilee*. Sometimes, Derek plays loud opera music, and sometimes I bang on the ceiling with a broom handle, and shout, '*Shut up!*', when the music gets so loud I can't concentrate. Derek is always friendly when he passes me on the stairs, with his boyfriend – a handsome Frenchman – both of them wearing black leather. Going home at night, walking down the dark, concrete stairway, exotic people are walking up, pushing past me. These are Derek's actors who I wrongly take to be guests arriving for a party.

I've taught myself to type; three years after art school, and with no sign of any lucrative employment, I buy a teach yourself to type book in Foyles, by Charles M. Smith: *A Practical Course in Touch Typing*, together with a cheerful yellow portable typewriter. The book has a deep purple cover, and you flip the pages over, vertically, like a writing pad, as you go through it. When you finish, you turn the pad over and resume on the other side:

> *Dear Sir,*
> *I enclose an advertisement taken from tonight's Post, and am amazed to learn that the people of your town are allowing outside parties to get control of so much valuable property in the suburbs.*
> *Will you kindly look up these lots and let me know whether, in your opinion, the extravagant claims as to their value are justifiable?*
> *Yours faithfully,*

The letters are complete gobbledy-gook as far as I'm concerned – from another time, another era – and I am too impatient to learn numbers, so I never manage to get to the end of the book. I don't think I'll have much use for numbers anyway.

I walk into the little gallery, which is located in a mews behind Tottenham Court Road, and say, 'Have you got any work? I can type.' Angela takes me on the spot – doesn't even want a reference, and she doesn't seem to mind my stammer either. Angela is kind, although with her grey Armani suits, and short blonde hair, she presents a brusque exterior. A perfectionist with an eye for detail, she can spot a typo or spelling error a mile off – or a smudge on a badly washed wine glass. On the other hand, she bakes her own bread, at home on an Aga, surrounded by an enormous brood of children – mostly boys, and an assortment of cats.

I never sell much – the occasional postcard, or (on a good week), a rainbow screen-print by Patrick Hughes. Once, during a sculpture exhibition, someone even steals a small ceramic baby, leaving an empty space on its ceramic pillow on top of the plinth.

Amazingly a decade passes between leaving Summerhill and putting down roots. In the end I find a home in a street of ramshackle short-life houses in Hackney. My next-door neighbour, Vi, who is in her fifties, and was born in her house, says the street was 'a lovely turning' in the old days – before the council started moving everyone out and into high rise flats. I imagine women in pinnies, scrubbing their doorsteps, and window boxes with flowers decorating the now crumbling window sills.

A railway bridge divides the street in half: the bridge I travelled over as a ten-year-old, on my way to Summerhill. Pebble-dashed brick houses lead off the main road up to the bridge and then, on the other side – framed and divided by the arch and underpass of the bridge – stands the other half of the terrace, where the pebble-dash has run out. This is where the artists live, in twenty-six of the houses (no heating and outside loos). Front doors open onto the pavement, so the street has the look of a Northern working class street of back-to-backs.

We seem to be in and out of each other's houses all the time, borrowing milk, sugar, paint, ladders… The street is so quiet, that we play badminton in the middle of the road at the weekends. In the summer, we bring chairs out to the fronts of the houses and read the Sunday papers. When the sun comes out, we sit on each other's doorsteps, drinking tea, taking a break from whatever we're doing, parents watching their children ride up and down the pavement on skateboards, bicycles, rollerblades, making sure they don't stray too far.

I love my studio at the top of the house; it faces south, and is always full of light. I've knocked the wall through from the front to the back, so it's L-shaped, with two front windows looking out over the street, and, at the back, one big sash window, overlooking Vi's rambling roses in the summer and, beyond the garden wall, a wasteland of weeds, fenced in by corrugated iron, where once there were more houses like ours.

They are already living across the street when I arrive – the problem family. There are no curtains on the windows, so you can see inside – three little blond children in dirty vests. The floor – beautifully sanded and varnished, with a black border painted around it; junk-yard sofas and, for some reason, a grand piano. Shouting in the night – a man's voice yelling, 'let me in', heavy pounding, glass breaking, empty milk bottles tumbling over on the pavement.

Sometimes, the father comes over to my house and borrows money, sugar or milk. He has the same dark good looks as my father, but I am wary of him. The two eldest children, Charlie and his sister, Rose get into the habit of coming to play after school. They make drawings in my studio. Sometimes we write messages to each other and hold them up to the window. Charlie writes: 'Hello Mikey, we are here.' I write: 'Hello Charlie, I like your blue pullover,' in blue paint on a sheet of cartridge paper, or 'Time for Tea', with a drawing of a teapot.

The woman (their mother) comes over to my house with a black eye, her sticky baby girl clutched to her side, to use the phone; she leaves, in a taxi, with a laundry bag and the baby. The husband comes round in a grubby yellow jumper, and cries and cries. I give him a bath, and a clean shirt – one that belongs to an old boyfriend who is living in America now.

I start looking after the children; they come round to wait for their father to return from college. We make scones in the kitchen (Rose, the youngest, doesn't like raisins in hers). They each have a favourite cup – Charlie's a tiny Suzie Cooper with orange polka dots painted around it, and Rose's a little wavy one – white with gold highlights that sits on a wavy saucer. I put mostly milk in their tea. They are starving all the time.

They sit in my studio, on the floor, surrounded by pastels and crayons, and make drawings in pages torn from my sketchbook. Rose draws princesses, in flouncy, bouffant evening gowns; Charlie draws the two of them – himself and Rose – adrift on a pencilled ocean in a boat, the mast, with a banner on it saying 'To Mikey', and the sky, an upside down horizon in heavy dark blue. Something in me – unspoken – acknowledges the link to my own childhood: they are waiting for their mother to come and rescue them.

My lovely cousin Jeanne Murray, who married Alfred Vanderbilt, comes to visit – I meet her in the West End, and she takes me out for tea somewhere fancy. Contact with the American family is like a smash and grab. I have a sense that the tea is done out of a sense of duty, that even Jeanne, who has never laid eyes on me before, feels responsible for our predicament, our exile, and that treating us to scones and cream might make things better, soothing us with sugar and china teacups.

When my Uncle Lester comes to visit with Aunt Gabby and Little Les, they bring a turkey from Harrods – to Hackney. Gabby gets to work in my kitchen, cooking up a beautiful Thanksgiving dinner. She has just begun to lose her recent memory, and every once in a while she wonders out loud, 'Have we put the turkey in the oven yet?'

1978: the summer after the Queen's Silver Jubilee, I fly back to New York on Laker Airways. My little sister Nanette is living with my stepfather in Southampton, in a beautiful old house on Hill Street, and running a small bed and breakfast. People from the city rent a room for the summer, and come down for weekends, sitting at the kitchen table in the morning for large, communal breakfasts. Nanny makes everyone feel wonderfully at home.

My sister and I go to the Southampton beach club with some friends and sit on the hot expensive sand, a stars and stripes fluttering in the Atlantic breeze. We watch Jackie O, recognizable in her sunglasses, walk along the shore, barefoot, deep in conversation with her daughter Caroline.

I take photos of Sean playing baseball for a roofing company he's working for over the summer. He's wearing a green T-shirt with 'I'm Proud to be Irish' written, misspelt and crossed out several times before it comes right. Pat, his wife and her little girl Rachel – from a previous relationship, are watching from the bleachers. He's happy. So what goes wrong?

I hear the news from my sister Deedee. She is always the purveyor of news between the siblings; she never falls out with any of us.

'Wow, I just heard from Sean. He's split up with Pat, and Chris has moved in with her!'

'My God. Poor Sean; what's he going to do now? And what about Margaret and the boys?'

Chrissy has been with Margaret and her two children for ten years, ever since he went home with her after a New Year's Eve party in Notting Hill when he was sixteen. She was twenty-nine. He claims he thought Margaret was a one-night stand. They got married in 1973, not long after his nineteenth birthday. When he turned twenty-one, he adopted her two boys.

'Oh, that's been over for a while. That's why Chris went over to Southampton – to think things over.'

So, now there's a rift between my brothers that, in spite of Sean's one and a half marriages since then, and the fact that Chris and Pat have stayed together and have a grown-up son, has never properly healed. It's common knowledge that Pat was on the verge of throwing Sean out when Chrissy arrived. I imagine Sean drinking beers (on the couch) all day, and watching TV, gambling at the track, and ignoring Pat and her little girl.

When my little brother appears, gallant and energetic, Pat is bowled over and that, as they say, is that.

Chapter 27

I'm at my brother's place in Edinburgh visiting from London for the Christmas holidays. Margaret Thatcher is a few months into her second term as prime minister after a landslide victory in June. Greenham Common peace camp is all over the news. An IRA car bomb has exploded in Oxford Street; no one's been injured. Bob is interviewing Margaret Thatcher for a television news programme about Alec Douglas-Home. They are sitting with a table and two glasses of water between them. My brother is *definitely* looking forward to something stronger after the programme.

'Mrs Thatcher, could you give me your thoughts about Sir Alec Douglas-Home, and his contribution to the Conservative party?'

My brother with wide lapels and sideburns, hair luxuriant, looks slightly embarrassed. Margaret in a pussy-bow blouse looks young, attractive even. She's as cool as a cucumber. Later Bob will tell me that she made no reference to the night before when, at the end of a boozy evening at the Station Hotel during the Conservative party conference in Perth, she had sat on the arm of my brother's chair and almost toppled over. It had been up to my brother to put a restraining hand on her knee to 'save' her.

Bob, who has studied politics and economics in Edinburgh with half the future Labour cabinet, is Scotland's glamorous, trans-atlantic voiced political correspondent. (*Scotland's answer to Walter Cronkite*, runs the family joke). As a student, he chaired the Viet-nam Solidarity Campaign and chartered buses to London for demos outside the American embassy. Now he's an all-expenses-paid correspondent, hobnobbing with the people he once scorned.

His study is plastered with photos of himself and the roll-call of politicians he interviews over the years, before he is eventually ousted by a younger incumbent. I re-examine them every time I go to visit. In each shot Bob looks less and less like his former self. Even Nixon, looking like a waxwork, is too real to be true; and there's Kissinger, talking to my brother like they're old friends. Kissinger. Wow Bob.

In the early days, when he's in London on business, Bob phones and tries to persuade me to come and join him and his researcher and friend at the Basil Hotel in Knightsbridge for dinner. I haven't been living in London for long. I always decline. I know that Bob will get drunk and above himself, snapping his fingers at waiters, making inappropriate remarks to waitresses. I can't bear it.

His researcher's name is Gordon Brown. Bob is in fact trying to fix me up with Gordon. I'm not sure whether he's doing it for Gordon's sake or his own. One Easter, when I've come up to Edin-burgh on holiday from art school in London, Gordon and I have a date in Edinburgh in a fancy-mirrored pub in Rose Street. Gordon, a brilliant political raconteur even then, always wears a suit (or at least a tie). Even as a Student Union rep at university, his hair is never over long and he always wears a smart jacket, never looks as dishevelled as the others.

Standing in the beautiful, mirrored pub in Rose Street, his clever wit is lost on me. I find him dull. And what does Gordon think of me? Perhaps he finds me exotic, maybe even beautiful, but I'm too skittish for his liking, and I have nothing to say with my dreadful stammer. I am nice to look at, but a little flouncy and eccentric for his tastes in my Biba maxi coat and second-hand dress.

It becomes obvious that Gordon prefers Margarita, a fellow student, studying Sociology at Edinburgh University. Margarita has the good looks and dress sense of a trendy Scottish lassie, plucked eyebrows, mini skirts and leather boots, and she has wit and 'breeding'. She is, after all, a princess. Her father, reportedly a bus driver in Geneva, is the deposed King of Romania, and Margarita's education is being paid for by the Queen. We are all a bit intimidated by Margarita's credentials, but there is no need; she is lovely and down to earth.

I meet up with Gordon some years later at a party in Edinburgh, at the Scottish National Gallery. Gordon, now a key player in the shadow cabinet, comes bounding up to me (kiss kiss). With his fame, he seems more handsome, confident, and in charge of social proceedings than when I last met him. There are no silences to fill. I wear a borrowed suit from my niece, Aimee, working a gap year in Wallis on Princes Street. Gordon, trying to give himself more height (at five foot ten I am taller than him in my high heels) raises himself endearingly up onto the skirting board on his tippy toes.

One of the museum guards asks him to, 'Move away from the Tintoretto.' Before we part, he tells me I must come and visit him in Fife, but we both know I never will.

Chapter 28

Evie, Sally and I have come to see Ulla. She's been living in Berlin since her retirement. It's May 1990 and the city is leafy and optimistic. Street traders are selling brightly coloured pieces of the Berlin Wall, priced according to size, spread out on blankets on the pavement. Even in the airport souvenir shop, they are selling tiny relics of the wall in plastic boxes, and then huge bits with panoramas of the wall behind, set in plastic with barbed wire threaded through; the epitome of kitsch, but I buy one anyway.

Evie is writing an article about Ulla for the Summerhill newsletter and Sally and I have been invited to come along. Evie picks me up at my house and drives us to the airport. I sit next to her, watching her drive – examining her profile, and her face, turned towards me every once in a while for emphasis – her lizard lidded eyes, a smattering of freckles across her nose, the short, pixie hair cut. It's great to see her.

'How's Myrtle?'

'Don't ask', she says looking straight ahead.

I know a little bit about her resentments; being abandoned at Summerhill at the age of four so her mother could go busking around Europe with a skiffle group. Then, of course, there was Chrissy who used to tease and bully her with his, 'Your mum loves *me* more than you.'

I'm mortified when she tells me this.

I feel responsible somehow. If only I'd known. But even when Evie voices her resentments, she smiles at them as if they are her very own beloved naughty children. I can't imagine her having dark thoughts.

I have a friend who has agreed to put us up in his studio in an old convent in Kreutzberg. The studio is white and spacious, with wooden floorboards, and big windows. We sleep on three little mattresses, side by side. It feels like school, the dormitory all over again, and we stay up late, chatting through the night. Sally and Evie sit leaning against the wall, smoking cigarettes, wearing their sleeping bags like strapless evening dresses.

Ulla lives in a leafy suburb, her childhood home. We spend the weekend visiting her. It feels like a piece of jigsaw has been put into place, being able to picture her, finally in this setting, this Grillparzerstrasse 5 where I've been sending letters and parcels since her retirement in 1970. At the age of eighty-five, Ulla climbs the four flights of stairs to her flat with ease, Evie, Sally and myself trailing behind.

The flat is like a slightly larger version of her room at school with the same inimitable smell of cinnamon and allspice. It almost feels as if I am back at Summerhill. Ulla and I hug each other in the kitchen. She feels so small – frail – and I can't help crying. Everything is so familiar, not strange at all, as if this is what I've been missing, without knowing it, until now. We take her out the next day to her favourite Italian bistro around the corner. We sit outside on white, curly metal chairs, the tables covered in red fabric tablecloths. She is alarmingly thin, and obliges us by eating a bowl of spaghetti, with a glass of red wine, and then a tiramisu. She is wearing a blouse I vaguely recognize, pale blue, edged in lace, over a pair of trousers, and she points out that it is in fact a nightie I had sent her the Christmas before last, from Marks & Sparks, which she has cut down to wear as a blouse.

'*Naja*, I could not waste such a beautiful object on myself and the bed sheets,' she explains to me.

We aren't her only visitors. Ulla has a huge fan base, ex-Summerhillians and parents who she corresponds with on a regular basis. Sometimes, forgetting her decades, she writes,

> *Oh, I had a letter from Renate last week; she's doing well and*
> *so is the baby. Or, Gerda and Jonathan visited me this summer;*
> *they were travelling by car, driving all the way from their home in*
> *Wales, and we went out to the country with a picnic…*

I have no idea who Renate, Gerda, or Jonathan are.

I return home and continue to receive Ulla's letters in her spidery, German handwriting, the microscopic writing designed to save paper, which is as thin as air to save on postage costs. In many ways, the letters, and what they contain are less important than the letters themselves, which constitute a declaration of interest; a sign of devotion.

In return, I write and tell Ulla everything.

I just want to find someone to make me happy, I confide in her. She writes back.

Mein Liebling,

… Happiness belongs to the self-sufficient (to quote a famous philosopher), meaning that it comes from within. You won't find it in another. You must look to yourself for that. Remember I used to say to you typies, whenever one or other of you were feeling disheartened, 'one swallow does not a summer make,' and you always looked a little non-plussed? (That was from Aristotle too). It means that happiness is not a fleeting, transitory thing; rather it occupies an entire lifetime.

Her advice doesn't end here. Taking into account my damaged background, she advises me never to have children. I have my own welfare to look after, my career as an artist, and that's going to be difficult enough, *without a little one to look after as well.* My heart sinks at this last bit of advice. I have always wanted children.

Over the following year or two, her letters become infrequent, the writing shakier. Then no Christmas card. No answer to the anxious and foreign-sounding 'beep beep' when I telephone.

I receive a letter, in unfamiliar handwriting, bordered in black.

It's from some cousins of Ulla, Klauss and Brigitte, telling me that Ulla has died. It was what I expected. Ulla had gone already when her letters stopped. I cry, and feel remorse. I had just let her go, let her slip from my grasp, float away. Why didn't I do more? Why was I so feeble in my efforts to contact her?

I get a friend to translate the letter. I send flowers from all of us and a letter translated into German to tell them how much Ulla meant to me and my friends. Some time later, I receive a parcel. I open it to find some chocolates and a patchwork quilt. The quilt spills out from the paper. Ulla hasn't quite finished it and Klauss and Brigitte hope I don't mind that they have sent it to me as it was.

I back the quilt in some of my own fabric and put a border around it, not quite as carefully as Ulla might have wished. I'm in a hurry and I lay it on my son's bed to keep him warm. I smile when I look at the patches of material, the humour in their juxtaposition, some patches, horrid Crimplene, others 1930s nursery, all hoarded and saved with care. Each piece of fabric has a history, a story behind it, which I can only imagine. I would love to have known what those stories were; how all those bits of fabric connected.

I wonder if I loved Ulla. How will I ever know? I realize now, perhaps too late, that I never dared love a soul in that place.

Chapter 29

Between us we have eight children. Bob has three (two girls and a boy), Deedee has two (a boy and a girl), and Chrissy, Nanette and I have a boy each. Sean has none that he knows of. James, my son, is the youngest. It took me longest to get there, past the age my mother was when she died at thirty-eight. A 38-year-old myself, I finally recognize that someone gentle and supportive at my side might be a good bet, that living in a permanent state of conflict with someone isn't conducive either to my work, or my hopes for a child, a family.

I am a month and a half from turning forty when I have James, by emergency caesarean section after a thirty-hour labour, at the Homerton Hospital in Hackney. Mercy is the community midwife from Ghana. I am her last job before she retires. She reminds me of Vidy. She's keen to get to the doctor's surgery for the Christmas party, so she hands me over to the hospital, after my partner and I have tried for quite a few hours for a home delivery. She stays in touch with us (it's her job), and writes a beautiful card which she puts through our door one day when we are out, referring to James as *King James the First.*

I don't remember much about the labour, except that I wanted my mother, and I cried out for her.

It's Christmas at Deedee's flat in Glasgow, and she has cooked the dinner with turkey and all the trimmings, including mashed sweet potatoes with melted marshmallows on top, just like Mom used to make. Not one to stand on ceremony, Deedee has provided tartan paper plates with matching napkins, and plastic wine glasses for the cava. The plates are a little soggy from the gravy. Omar, my sister's budgie, hops around the table, helping himself to titbits.

'Look what I've got,' she says, after we've done the washing up.

It's my grandmother's passport from 1927. She'd gone on a European tour, by ship, with my grandfather, leaving their children behind. My cousin Les has put a carefully typed note, on a small white piece of card, so that it will fit inside.

Dear Deedee,

I thought you might like this. Our grandmother looks nice here. (She is wearing a black cloche hat) ... *I think it is before she had Bell's palsy. It killed the muscles in her face. She traveled on her husband's passport. Women lived in civil inattention, but within the law. More later. Love to all, Less III.*

'Bell's palsy?' I look at my sister who shrugs.

Thinking of my grandmother's unreadable expression – realizing she was unable to smile, even if she wanted to – I feel devastated for her. But, as always, we are the last to know.

The phone rings and my sister brings it to the table.

'He wants to speak to you', she says.

'Who is it?'

Tom. She mouths the name.

I pick up the phone.

'So, how have you been?' says Uncle Tom.

How have I been? I want to shriek, incredulous. *Where've you been for the past thirty years?* Doesn't he know about the private detectives, the tortuous family conversations that skirt the topic of Tom without resting on a subject no one feels brave enough to broach? We have a careful, gentle exchange. Uncle Tom sounds the same, but a bit older, with the same refined Manhattan twang as his siblings – the soft 'r's and slightly flat vowel sounds. He says he will write.

I put the phone down, shaking.

'Why has he suddenly got in touch, after all these years?'

'I guess he finally got away from the *Sullivanians,*' says Deedee in a mock drawl.

'The who…?'

Sullivanians sounds a little like Sylvanians, those miniature plastic animals that little girls are so fond of. I can just imagine flock-covered rabbits and bears living together in a yellow and pink plastic house, with miniature furniture, and a handle on the roof to carry it around with.

'You know, those people who were always hanging around with Tom in his apartment. They weren't there by accident. They all lived together, like a cult. That guy Saul was their leader.'

'How do you know so much about it?' I say, although actually I'm not surprised. Deedee always knows ten times more than me about most things.

'Uncle Les dug it up. The Sullivanians were persuaded by their leader, Saul, who agreed to father a child with Joan, remember, to break all ties with their families and regard the "Group" as their new family. Parents were discouraged from bringing up their own children or living as a family unit…'

'My God.'

I'm in shock.

'Someone wrote a big exposé on them in *New York Magazine*. I've got a copy of it somewhere. Uncle Les sent it to me years ago.'

She goes to the big chest of drawers in her bedroom where various documents and treasures are kept.

'Here it is.' She passes it over.

My uncle (the letter's dated 1976) writes:

Dear Deedee,

For a while, I hesitated to send this to you, because Tom is my brother. I do love him and I know that you do too. For a long time all of us have wondered about Tom's behavior. That is, we wondered how to explain it. Now Tom is my brother, and a wonderful fellow, but there have been times when I wondered what really made him tick. A fellow named David Black finally wrote an article called 'Totalitarian Therapy on the Upper West Side'. Your Uncle Jack and I think Tom belongs, or did belong to this group… This article may help explain some of his actions. Back in the early fifties when I was going to a psychiatrist for a while I went to a man named Saul B. Newton. Tom went to his wife Dr Jane Pearce. I think I stopped seeing Saul B. Newton back in 1953. I have good memories of him. Apparently after I left or some time after I left, Saul B. Newton started or created something new that seemed to grow into a successful group. When I knew Saul Newton he was still married to Dr Jane Pearce. Then they published a book. Well, at any rate read on and enjoy.

By the way, Tom sounded happy and reasonably healthy when I last caught up with him. He had a very good job for a while working for the office of the ageing in New York. Then when the city went practically bankrupt he lost his job. He got a job working in the jewelry department at R.H. Macy's during the Christmas vacation, then he went straight to a new job in Honesdale, Pennsylvania, working at an institution that rehabilitates alcoholics.

I reluctantly unfold the article from *New York Magazine*:

TOTALITARIAN THERAPY ON THE UPPER WEST
SIDE
by David Black

I just received a blackmail threat from a therapist I went to for six weeks. She belongs to the Sullivanian community of therapists and patients who live close to each other on the Upper West Side of Manhattan. Earlier this evening I called her to tell her I was writing an article about the Sullivanian movement and to ask if we could meet to talk about the group. She asked why I wanted to talk to her.

I told her that my short experience with her had been reasonably pleasant. She had seemed a sympathetic, friendly, intelligent therapist. I couldn't square my impressions of the Sullivanian movement with the grim tales I'd been hearing – rumors of kidnapping children of members who were trying to sever ties with the group, of purges, of institutionalized paranoia, of venomous hostility to anyone who threatened to breach the circle of secrecy surrounding the group.

I wanted to ask her how she thought the group had come to develop such an unsavory reputation. … Estimates of the (Sullivanian) group's size vary from 350 to 600 members. There are approximately forty therapists (who are also patients of one another); and, since each therapist can theoretically handle up to twenty patients, the community may very well number as many as 800 – although not all of them are part of the inner circle, members who live with and socialize exclusively with each other.

… The members of the group's inner circle started sharing apartments in the early 1960s as much for economic reasons as for ideological ones. Now, in many of the apartments, members live in barracks. When they have sleep-over dates, they sign up for the apartment's date room, 'a sex room' as one former member described it.

During the summer, the Sullivanians migrate to a commune at Barnes Landing near Amagansett; when they travel abroad, they travel in packs. Members with children are pressed into hiring nurses and au pairs to help. 'If you don't have a full-time baby sitter and if you don't send your kids to private school,' said an ex-Sullivanian, 'they say you hate your kids.'

… Sullivanians who feel they were weaned improperly wander around sucking on pacifiers. Sullivanians who feel they missed out on the experience of hanging around with pals go out and cultivate adolescent-type friendships. Even more important than recapitulating infant cuddling, breast-feeding, and adolescent pal-ships is duplicating the experience of living within a family. Not the old destructive family – it is Sullivanian dogma that all families (all non-Sullivanian families) are destructive; all parents, especially all mothers, are monsters – but a new healthy, supportive family of Sullivanian therapists and patients.

To make this new family experience work, one must free oneself from blood relatives, a painful process not only for the Sullivanian patient, but also for the patient's kin who are being abandoned…

I put the article down.

'Why've you never shown me this before?'

'I didn't see the point.'

'How could Tom do that? Send us all away and then disappear?'

'He was *told* to send us away,' Deedee tries to explain.

I feel a huge wave of emptiness wash over me. It's a version of the truth that I haven't been prepared for. It's horrible. Sick.

'I always thought there was something heroic about Tom,' I try to make sense of it. 'Taking us on like that, and even sending us to Summerhill was kind of inspirational. But now, he just seems weak. I mean, he was just following orders, wasn't he?'

My sister shrugs.

'I guess so. The evidence is pretty stacked against him.'

'What about the custody battle?'

She gives me a look. 'We all know there was never really any custody battle. I mean, Grandma put up a bit of a fight in the beginning, but it was decided, probably between her and Uncle Les, that it was easier in the end to leave us here, and *cheaper*.' She laughs. 'Tom couldn't or wouldn't provide a home for us, anyway. I mean, he'd run out of money, and he was mentally screwed up, wrapped up in all that Sullivanian psychobabble. And Grandma must have winced at the idea of us, raising havoc in her apartment…'

'So, in reality,' I say to Deedee, 'we were kind of dumped here.'

'Yup, you've got it.'

The first letter from Uncle Tom arrives early in the New Year, with a fat, hopeful thud on my doormat. He is living in New Hampshire, semi-retired, and writing for a local paper. The envelope is crowded with stamps on the front, some with love heart logos saying I ♥ you, and later, ones with daffodils.

He writes, *Dear Elizabeth, It was good to talk to you after all these years…*

His letter is quite brief, two pages, but he encloses a xeroxed four-page résumé, cataloguing his career to date, from Harvard to The Bank of New York, to his work with various clinics as a child psychologist. There are photos too: a sweet-looking teenage boy and girl on a mountain top, who I examine for a family likeness; another of a Korean couple, and one of a wedding, but I don't recognize anyone. He has xeroxed an article he'd written for the local paper on moose kill statistics. There is a graph too, which he's designed.

PROBLEMS WITH MOOSE ON 1-93
by Tom Cuddihy

In the graph presented here, between 1998–2003, there were 39 moose motor vehicle collisions from Exit 34c on 1-93 to Exit 37. On the Route 141 and Route 3, part of the graph that includes 1093 on the Southwest side, there were a further 12 collisions.

(And so on.)

We ring each other a few times, but our conversations are awkward, the echo of my voice, the beat of silence between our two voices, exaggerates the gap that exists between us and can never be filled. There are a few more letters over that year, and more photos, a funny one of him with a glove puppet (a comic and strange looking crow); another of him dressed in a choir outfit in church.

In one of his final letters, he encloses a photo of Uncle Jack sitting with his wife, Heidi, on the top step outside their apartment building. They have lived all their married life in this brownstone in Greenwich Village. Their three grown-up children and a clutch of grandchildren are spread out on the steps below them. It's summer and they are all wearing white. The children are barefoot.

Examining the photo, I feel a kind of fascinated envy and for the first time, I have the notion that perhaps I've missed out on something. A life that Uncle Tom could've given us, sitting on the steps of our very own brownstone, together, had he been so inclined.

There's an unspoken belief in my family that once upon a time we owned Manhattan. We had shares in it. We'd been a part of it since the first foundations were laid. It's not so much a sense of entitlement exactly, but more that our family's history is integral to the city's history. Seeing this family photograph, I wonder if we, my brothers, sister and myself, are still a part of the city's history and its pioneering spirit. Ford, Edison, Funk and Wagnalls, Vanderbilt… Whenever I hear these names, I feel a sense of distant pride, a connection with the scions of America that we once had, but somehow lost along the way.

Lost. I write back to Tom, hinting gently at my feelings about it all, but he seems to take it badly. His final letter, written on a thin piece of paper, torn from a notebook, or ledger, addresses me as:

My dear Mikey,
I am sorry that you still long for that which you can never have,
namely a family that appears all together in the photo that I sent
you. However, here you are making suggestions about what all this
togetherness means, and here you could be way off.

… and later,

I think quite frankly that your comments about not being a family
and missing all those family things really got to me – I'm sorry
Mikey, but I did the best I could at the time, and I couldn't do it
differently.

When he rings the following Christmas, which I am spending at home in London, I don't pick up the phone. I listen later to his feeble, 'Merry Christmas', feeling a little ashamed.

I don't phone him back.

Chapter 30

I hear the news on my radio in the studio. I want to run to my son's school and get him, hold him close to me. I go downstairs and put the TV on and watch the second tower being crashed into. Watching this horror unfold. Oh the poor people. My city, wrecked, dismembered. Where are my family? Are they OK?

I suddenly feel completely American. More than that, I am a *New Yorker*. I feel like I did when I was a child at Summerhill. I want to be there, with my American family.

In the days that come with the sky silent, I want to put a flag in my window, hang the stars and stripes from a flagpole, but I don't. I daren't. I search for my cousin Lester, for my cousins and my aunts and uncles on the newsreels, showing the streets of Manhattan, the shocked faces. Everyone I know is OK. Chrissy and his colleagues at work have lost friends, partners, children. He has been crying on and off all week.

I call all my siblings.

'Have you seen…?'

'Can you believe it…?'

Two years later, I return to New York with my son James. My brother Chris (as I've learn to call him) collects us from the airport, and drives us out to his and Pat's home in Hampton Bays, on Long Island. The beach in Hampton Bays is crowded with people who look like the cast from *The Sopranos*. The man to my left with a hairy chest and gold medallion is a dead ringer for Tony S. He's yelling at his kids. People are diving into the gentle waves and there is all that lovely sand, and sky writers, the putter putter of an airplane engine, writing love messages in the air.

I feel at home here.

At my brother's house, I run my hand across the dining-room table and benches familiar from our childhood and rescued from Larry's garage. My sister, Nanny, drives us to Montauk, where we swim in the sea; it's calmer and a bit pebbly. There are preppy-looking New Yorkers with paler skin and thinner bodies dipping their children into the waves, and gingerly lifting them out again. We take a walk around the big historic houses in Sag Harbour, and then drive past the Barn in Watermill; my sister doesn't remember the mansion or the pool.

Back to feed Lucky, my sister's dog, at the house where she lives with her eighteen-year-old son, Wesley, who in six week's time (although neither of us knows this yet) will come to live with us in London and go to art school.

Nanny's house is beautifully clean, with lovely arrangements of books and old kitchen utensils. Before I leave, she gives me her own vintage copy of *The Joy of Cooking*. I read the inscription she's written when I'm on my own, and it makes me cry.

Chris, after years of back-breaking jobs, cleaning swimming pools, digging roads, building brick walls, and various other enterprises, has gone back to school and trained as a systems analyst. He's doing well. He has his own business and a job, with health insurance.

A family man, he has embraced Pat's huge family and my sister Nanny. He is even in regular contact with my stepfather Larry's children and all the relatives in Manhattan. He has dogs, a big yard and tattoos on both his arms that surprise me. A fortieth birthday present from Pat, he tells me.

He is aggressively friendly. On a bus, a plane, a train, he will speak to all the passengers. Like Bob, he talks incessantly but his talk is social, about people and things that have happened to him. He's argumentative, provocative. Exhausting. He never stops. He works hard at self-improvement. He faces his fears. He is born again, and he doesn't drink anymore. As a father, when his son and his stepdaughter were small, he was a strict disciplinarian. I used to worry that he was too strict, but his family adore him.

Sometimes he goes too far. He makes pronouncements that can be wincingly final. He has quite a high voice, in contrast to my brother Sean, who speaks in a deep baritone.

On a recent visit to New Hampshire, where he has been visiting my long lost Uncle Tom, driving back with Little Les in the car, he has a go at him. He phones to tell me about it:

'I just said to him, you know Les, you are such a fuck-up. Why don't you do something about your life, instead of bitching about everything all the time? Get off your fucking ass and sort yourself out!'

Whereupon Les gets out of the car and catches the train home to the city.

Chris's wife Pat is serene, calm, held down a steady job for years; allows Chris to be the loud one, the risk-taker. She doesn't argue, she negotiates around him. She is perfect; she's a diplomat. And she's beautiful.

Chris puts his energy into extreme sports challenges, raising money for charities. He rows the South Atlantic with three other men in a 30-foot trimaran. It takes thirty-six days. He is terrified of enclosed spaces, and they have to spend their rest periods in the cabin below, which is like a coffin.

He is showing me the blisters on his feet, from a thirty-three-hour marathon, which are painted with iodine. We talk about Summerhill, the old days.

'Have you seen anything of Myrtle or Evie?' he asks.

'Yes. I went to a poetry reading, and Myrtle was reading some of her poems. I've got the book somewhere. Here it is.' I pull it out of my bag.

He flicks through the pages.

'Ha!'

'What?'

'"In Praise of Young Men." Now that's funny.'

'Why?'

'I *was* one of Myrtle's young men.'

'What do you mean?' The question sticks in my throat.

'She used to come down to Summerhill and have sex with me.'

'You're kidding.'

'She wasn't the first. There was that housemother who taught English, you know, Judith, with the pointy glasses. Christ, she just wouldn't leave me alone. I hated it.'

With the pointy glasses? The wife of the woodwork teacher?

I stare at him in disbelief, remembering him slapping away her groping hands: *Get off me.*

'Why didn't you say? Why didn't you tell anyone?'

'Well, I told Myles about Judith, but... Anyway, what would anyone have done? I thought it was, you know, free love and all that.'

'We all knew about Myles and his penchant for young girls, but I thought he was just an aberration.'

'An *aberration*? Is that what you call it?'

'You know what I mean. I didn't think...'

'Well, anyway, no harm done. Look, here I am all in one piece. OK, so I have to take a Valium every once in a while, but otherwise I'm as solid as a rock.'

I express my shock, my sadness that I never knew, he never confided in me, with silence.

'Don't worry about it,' he shrugs. 'I had some great times at

Myrtle's house. I used to go and stay with her in London. I got to go to jazz clubs, drink free beer all night and smoke fags. Sometimes I even got to shag my little brains out.' He laughs. 'I know it wasn't prudent of her, but it was welcomed by me. When I moved to London after Summerhill, she housed me and fed me, sat with me through the night just trying to calm my mind. The sex issue was such a short-lived bit of it. She did the best with what she had. I never felt taken advantage of, you know. But the housemother, boy, that wasn't very nice, although I did get some wanks out of it, and some dry humping in the hockey field.'

'Chrissy!'

'Out of all the people I spent time with, Myrtle was always consistent in her kindness. She treated me like a man.'

'But you weren't a man, you were a little boy who'd lost his mother.'

'I know, but remember, by fifteen I was living alone and had hitched from London to Scotland about half a dozen times. So it was OK. I had fun.'

And he laughs.

Saying goodbye, Chrissy bawls like a baby, his tears make a puddle on the ground, well almost. James and I get the Manhattan Jitney (an air-conditioned bus) into Manhattan. Driving the length of the island to the Upper East Side, James has his nose pressed against the window, looking up and up at the skyscrapers.

'Did you really live here, Mikey?' he says.

Chapter 31

I return to Hackney to find Sean sitting at my kitchen table. He's fleeing his second broken marriage left behind in California. He's put on weight, a huge amount, and is a terrible guest, tut-tutting at my son and his school friends who he regards as effeminate with their long hair and reluctance to talk about sport. He won't eat the food I cook, preferring burger and chips washed down with Coca-Cola from the local takeaway. He has come, as usual, with expensive presents, a camera and a Yankees baseball jacket for my son, and 'Sees' Candy for me.

He's nice to the cats.

Out of his luggage he produces a battered rolled-up piece of paper, brown with age and water damage. When I uncurl it, there is a portrait, in pastel, of our mother, which had hung framed over the mantelpiece when we were children in America. Mom is wearing a strapless eau de Nil coloured evening dress; her hands have worn away. I had always thought it was a painting. He has somehow retrieved it from Larry's garage in Southampton. The water damage has extended to my mother's hairline, and washed some of it away. She looks damaged, not like Mom at all, but I thank him, profusely, and try to remember the name of someone I once met who does paper restoration.

My brother casts a critical eye over my house, shaking his head at bare unpainted plaster, my cobbled together home-made kitchen; the cheap Ikea sofa bed, which he breaks.

I'm cooking supper and he's flicking through my copy of Herb Snitzer's photo book *Living at Summerhill*. It's the closest thing I have to a family album. Sean pauses to look at a photo. I look over his shoulder. It's of Sean speaking to Neill during Spontaneous Acting. Sean is looking up at him, pointing to himself, in mid-acting mode. It must have been towards the end of our first term. Sean's American crew cut is just growing out and his striped T-shirt is almost too small for him. He looks so animated. It's that first flicker of praise which Sean had so missed on arriving here without his baseball and soccer to excel in.

'I didn't know what the rules were at Summerhill,' he blurts out suddenly, without looking up. 'I mean, I did something bad to that little girl, but I didn't know I was doing anything wrong.'

'What do you mean?' I spin round, the half-peeled potato in my hand, half an ear listening to his rambling about the past; the unfairness of everything; his bewilderment at being packed off to England at the age of twelve, banished from all he loved and cherished; his Little League baseball, his English racing bike.

I feel sick, nearly faint with disbelief and realization. Of course, (mentally hitting myself on the forehead), why else would Sean have been expelled from Summerhill? You would have had to have done something pretty awful, something more than just locking a school friend in the toilet, to get thrown out. It had never added up.

'Oh Sean,' I manage.

Then Sean tells me what really happened all those years ago, as if the secret is a burden he has carried with him all this time and handing it to me might release him from its weight.

It started with some harmless chasing. Millie runs to the bathroom at the top of the stairs and tries to lock herself in, but Sean forces the door and locks it behind him. Millie doesn't stand a chance. She is little. He's a teenage boy. But she shouts and she screams, and eventually someone comes to the rescue – too late.

Ena had promised Sean that he wouldn't be thrown out no matter how badly he behaved. Then one day, not long after the Millie incident, he receives a shock. He is standing outside the back door by the kitchen, wearing his Southampton Mariners jacket and smoking a cigar that Esther, the grumpy grey-haired cook who never gives me anything, has given him, when Neill comes around the corner.

'Ah, Sean, I need to have a word with you. Can you come up to my office now?'

Sean stuffs the cigar into his pocket. He can smell it, smouldering away, burning a hole through the synthetic lining of his precious jacket.

Is this it?

'There's a train leaving Leiston at 4 p.m. for London,' Neill told him. 'Olly has packed your things for you. Harry will take you to London, and you will stay the night there and then he will put you on the train to Scotland in the morning. Now, dry your tears, laddie (he pats Sean on the back), and go and say goodbye to your pals.'

Apparently, the whole school came out to say goodbye. Some people were cheering, and others were crying. I don't remember a thing. Sean was at Summerhill one day and gone the next.

My heart goes out to my brother.

At the same time, a door closes between us.

I'll never be able to see him in the same light again as that poor wrongly accused teenage boy.

I try to extract something of the beautiful Sean from days gone by. I remember the last time he visited, ten years ago – with a new girlfriend. They were having a bit of an argument, and I went upstairs to the studio and put a Rolling Stones LP on the stereo full blast (Sean had bought it for me on a previous visit). He came upstairs and joined me, and we danced together, Sean strutting his stuff, so stylishly, so suavely, and miming to the words. Suddenly, everything was fine.

But even his eyes have lost their sparkle now. We search the house for his hipster belt. I had carefully put it away, and we can't find it – not even in the cupboard under the stairs, where everything forgotten seems to live.

Inevitably, we fight. I can't remember what about. There is a flash point, and I stomp off to the park in a temper, and phone Deedee to complain.

'He just sits there all day, watching TV, and staring at James and his friends when they get back from school, shaking his head. I know he thinks the house is a mess. He won't eat my food – no, nothing. Well, yes, cornflakes! We went out to the Turkish for dinner. He was furious that I was late. I mean, God, it was six o'clock for Chrissake. Who eats at six? You do? Oh, right! Well, he kept making jokes about Muslims under his breath. I'm sure the waiter heard. I bet they spat in our food. I was so embarrassed. What's wrong with him?'

I want him to go.

Finally he leaves.

I get a book down from my shelf, a thick hardback volume of collected correspondence, *All the best, Neill: Letters from Summerhill*. I've read the letter he wrote to John Aitkenhead, the headmaster at Kilquhanity, several times, and I know it almost by heart.

28th January 1964

Dear John & Morag,
S is a nice kid but he can't keep his finger out of other pies, hence a nuisance to younger ones, not so much bullying them by hitting, but annoying them till they get desperate. Sadly enough the others don't like him so that he spent a lot of time in the café in the town, where he was a bit of a nuisance, the owner said.

*Last term he tried to get into bed with bigger girls and they all
told him to go to hell. Then the story goes that he made a hysterical
girl of ten take down her knickers, also assaulted two other little
ones, all from America. Holidays, and hell let loose. The first
girl, M, a clever hysterical butchy kid, went home and told the
parents. Result cables, phone calls to me. She was kept at home.
Other parent, a psychiatrist, sent insulting cables about seduction.
S denies all. The other two girls tell me he never touched them, and
there he was speaking the truth to me. Dunno about M. He swears
nothing happened, but there must have been something. Over the
phone the hysterical mother screamed: My daughter was raped.
Oh, those bloody American parents. I've told the psychiatrist to
take his damn daughter home if he thinks she is going to be raped.*

*Poor S wept bitterly when I told him he was going. I am
really touched by your helping in this case. Maybe you can
succeed where we failed; maybe with his homelessness, his being
indoctrinated as an RC, the going will be hard, but he has a nice
side to him which you'll discover. I parted with him with real
sorrow (…)*

Love, Neill

I'm startled, once again, by Neill's vitriol towards 'those bloody
American parents', his bread and butter, but I'm touched by his
compassion for Sean. His insight. His comment on Sean's 'homelessness' stands out. He knew, he recognized it; he could see a need
that even Summerhill couldn't fill.

At the same time, I can only think of the lack of redress, the lack of empathy towards Millie, and how frightened she must have been.

That night I dig out a black and white photo of me aged eight or nine. I am standing, my body strangely rigid, blinking in the harsh, low winter sun, leaning against the Packard. Nanette is standing next to me on my right. She is only three and looks as if she's about to run out of the picture to somewhere more interesting. (She was always running off.)

I'm wearing a double-breasted, woollen coat, with a velvet collar, which is both too wide and too short for me, a hand-me-down from another child. The sleeves are too short, and the coat hangs on me like a bell, lifting at the front to show the hem of my dress. My legs are bare, stick-like, clad in ankle socks and scuffed shoes.

My right hand is slightly cupped, palm upwards. (What am I holding?) Shadow from a branch decorates my coat, darkens the roof of the car, then – sharper, more insistent in the windows – sweeps across the porch behind. My face looks long and angular, too grown up for an eight-year-old, but my sister says my legs look good.

It's only now, examining the photograph more closely, that I understand what's going on.

I can see clearly now that there are only two buttons holding my coat together. The third, the bottom button, is missing, my left hand gesturing to the gap where it once was. I'm holding that button in my cupped right hand, and I'm probably whining, not happy in the horrible ill-fitting coat, whining at my mother, wanting her to do something about the unattached button, because surely, that shadow in the foreground, taking the photo, that very feminine shadow, falling onto the grass in front of us, almost touching my feet, just has to be my mother.

I wonder if this isn't *the* Packard, and my mother's shadow, both in their final hours.

Perhaps we are on our way to my piano lesson.

My little sister will refuse to come and will stay at home.

Mom will drop me off and, later, I will wait in vain, on the corner of Main Street, outside the Presbyterian Church for her to pick me up.

She will never come.

Acknowledgements

Thanks to my agent, Jemima Hunt for taking this memoir on board, and for her indefatigable encouragement. Thanks to Margaret Stead, my publisher, who said she loved the book, and to Victoria Millar, my copy-editor. Thanks to Anna Linderstam – for reading and commenting on my very first draft, and to Catherine Johnson – for her wisdom and advice. Thanks to my beautiful niece, Rosita Murray, for her sharp eye and great feedback. A huge thank you to my sister, Deedee, for listening to me, for laughing at my jokes, and for all her stories. Thanks to Pete Smith, for the 'Conversation', and to Karen Knorr for her encouragement. Thanks to old Summerhillians Vicky Gregory and Hannah Byng for their enthusiasm, and to Cathy Baillie and Lenka Manning for their memories. A big thank you to my brothers, Bob, Sean, and Chris, for their version of events, and for giving me free reign to tell my story. Thanks to Sarah King and Gaby Koppel for their advice, and to many beloved friends and family who have helped along the way.

A Note on the Author

Born in New York, Mikey Cuddihy was educated at Summerhill School in Suffolk. She later studied fine art at Edinburgh College of Art and painting at Central School of Art and Design, and Chelsea College of Art. An art lecturer at the University of Brighton, Mikey is an acclaimed artist and writer.